Student Mastery Activities

to accompany

How to Design and Evaluate
Research in Education
Seventh Edition

Student Mastery Activities

to accompany

How to Design and Evaluate Research in Education
Seventh Edition

Jack R. Fraenkel
San Francisco State University

Norman E. Wallen
San Francisco State University

Boston   Burr Ridge, IL   Dubuque, IA   Madison, WI   New York   San Francisco   St. Louis
Bangkok   Bogotá   Caracas   Kuala Lumpur   Lisbon   London   Madrid   Mexico City
Milan   Montreal   New Delhi   Santiago   Seoul   Singapore   Sydney   Taipei   Toronto

The McGraw·Hill Companies

McGraw-Hill Higher Education

Student Mastery Activities to accompany
How to Design and Evaluate Research in Education
Jack R. Fraenkel and Norman E. Wallen

Published by McGraw-Hill, an imprint of The McGraw-Hill Companies, Inc., 1221 Avenue of the Americas,
New York, NY 10020. Copyright © 2009 by The McGraw-Hill Companies, Inc. All rights reserved.

1 2 3 4 5 6 7 8 9 0 QPD/QPD 0 9 8

ISBN: 978-0-07-332655-9
MHID: 0-07-332655-0

www.mhhe.com

TABLE OF CONTENTS

AUTHOR'S SUGGESTED ANSWERS TO ODD-NUMBERED QUESTIONS ... 167

PROBLEM SHEETS

CHAPTER 1: The Nature of Research

Activity 1.1: Empirical vs. Nonempirical Research

Activity 1.2: Basic vs. Applied Research

Activity 1.3: Types of Research

Activity 1.4: Assumptions

Activity 1.5: General Research Types

Activity 1.1:
Empirical vs. Nonempirical Research

Empirical research is research that involves the collection of firsthand information. Nonempirical research does not involve the collection of information at first hand. Thus, research that consists of locating and comparing references on a particular topic — the customary term paper — is not an example of empirical research. In *How to Design and Evaluate Research in Education,* we are concerned primarily with empirical research.

In the list of research topics that follows below, place an X in front of those that are examples of empirical research.

1. _____ A study of the effectiveness of a social learning program on the employability of severely disabled adults.

2. _____ The relationship between television watching and school achievement: a review of the literature.

3. _____ A reanalysis of the evidence on school effectiveness.

4. _____ The relationship between self-esteem and age at school entrance of fourth-grade students in the San Francisco Unified School District.

5. _____ Logical inconsistencies in writings of Sigmund Freud.

6. _____ A comparison of the effectiveness of behavior therapy as compared with client-centered therapy in homes for adolescent runaways.

Activity 1.2:
Basic vs. Applied Research

Listed below are a number of research projects that you can use to review your understanding of the distinction between basic and applied research. Place a "B" in front of those that you think are examples of basic research and an "A" in front of those that you think are examples of applied research.

1. _____ A comparison of the attitudes of different student ethnic groups toward the general education requirements at the City University of New York.

2. _____ The relationship between adolescent self-esteem and alcoholism in parents.

3. _____ A comparison of the effects of phonics versus look-say teaching on the achievement of Latino children in reading as based on the Amalo theory.

4. _____ Employer perceptions of changes in essential secretarial skills between 1945 and 1995.

5. _____ The effectiveness of counselors who are recovering alcoholics as compared with other counselors at the Rosewood Recovery Center.

6. _____ The effectiveness of using manipulative materials in teaching first-grade mathematics.

Activity 1.3:
Types of Research

What would be the most appropriate type of research to investigate each of the topics listed below? Match the letter of the appropriate research methodology from Column B with its topic in Column A.

Column A: Topic	Column B: Type of research
1. _____ Diplomatic relationships between Japan and the United States between 1918 and 1941.	a. A group-comparison experiment
2. _____ Images of women in U.S. history textbooks.	b. A survey
3. _____ Relationship between student attendance and achievement in chemistry classes.	c. A correlational study
4. _____ Number of single mothers on welfare in the city of Chicago.	d. A content analysis
5. _____ Daily activities of an operating room nurse in a big-city hospital.	e. A case study
6. _____ A comparison of the inquiry method and the lecture method in teaching high school biology.	f. An ethnography
7. _____ Changing impulsive behavior through the use of praise.	g. A historical study
	h. A single-subject experiment

Activity 1.4:
Assumptions

In this activity, you are to work with a partner to discuss what assumptions underlie each of the following statements:

1. "Spare the rod and spoil the child!"

_____
_____
_____
_____

2. "We couldn't beat McAteer High last season and we probably won't be able to beat them this year either."

_____
_____
_____
_____

3. "A stitch in time saves nine."

_____
_____
_____
_____

4. "Oh, brother, I have another one of the Johnson kids in my class next semester!!"

_____
_____
_____
_____

5. "Boy, I dread the thought of taking algebra from Mrs. West next semester!"

_____
_____
_____
_____

Activity 1.5:
General Research Types

Each of the following represents an example of one of the general research types we discussed in Chapter One in the text. Identify each as being either *descriptive, associational, or intervention* research.

1. A study of the possible relationship that may exist between class size and learning in remedial mathematics courses _____

2. A survey of the attitudes of parents in a large urban school district toward the advanced placement courses offered by the district _____

3. A study designed to compare the effectiveness of two methods of teaching spelling to first graders _____

4. An investigation by a researcher in an attempt to confirm that abstract concepts can be taught to six-year-olds _____

5. A historical study of high school graduation requirements _____

6. A detailed ethnographic study of the daily activities of a teacher in an inner-city high school _____

7. A comparison of inquiry and lecture methods of teaching 11th-grade history _____

8. A study designed to compare the attitudes of male and female students toward chemistry _____

CHAPTER 2: The Research Problem

Activity 2.1: Research Questions and Related Designs

Activity 2.2: Changing General Topics into Research Questions

Activity 2.3: Operational Definitions

Activity 2.4: Justification

Activity 2.5: Evaluating Research Questions

Activity 2.1:
Research Questions and Related Designs

Select the appropriate research design for each question listed below.

Case Study   Experimental
Causal-Comparative — *cause for differences*   Historical
Content Analysis   Surveys
Correlational — *relationships*   Ethnography — *cultures*
         2 populations

one pop → into 2 groups something divided up unevenly.

1. What do elementary school teachers in the San Francisco Unified School District think about full inclusion as practiced in their district?
    Survey

2. Is there a relationship between students' levels of social skills and successful transition into mainstream classes?
    Correlation

3. How do individuals with physical disabilities perceive themselves in comparison to their able-bodied peers in terms of work-related activities?
    Survey / Causal - Comparative
    ethnography

4. Does a whole-language curriculum lead to higher student achievement than a phonics curriculum?
    experimental / Correlation

5. How are teachers implementing the whole-language approach to reading in their curricula at Harding Elementary School?
    Case study

6. What were the key events that led to the demise of affirmative action in state hiring and college admissions in California?
    historical

7. How do magazines targeted at teenagers present information on safe-sex practices?
    Content analysis

8. Are the reasons Native American students give for dropping out of school different than those given by non-Native American Indian students?
    Ethnography

Causal Comparative — if all student dropouts.

Does a portfolio in which students provide evidence of meeting standards lead to more reflective learning?

8

Activity 2.2:
Changing General Topics into Research Questions

Change the following topics into researchable questions.

1. Class size and student achievement

2. Multicultural education at Thurgood Marshall Middle School

   memory

   If students take the same ~~test~~ *memory* three times in difference setting (dark room, right room, and light room *same student 3 tests over time 3 different cond. not light states*

   chewing gum.

3. Testing anxiety *students blood pressure d~~r~~op ~~e~~crease by at least 1%*

   Will ~~test scores increase~~ if lights are turned off during statewide ~~reading~~ test?   *feedback survey —*

4. Women college professors and tenure

   What is the relationship between w.c.p. reach tenure vs m.c.p. who reach tenure?

5. Alcohol consumption on New Year's Eve and Super Bowl Sunday

   Do people drink more on NYE vs SBS?
      ↳ Sales of alcohol
      → arrests

6. Single parents and affordable child care

   What is affordable child care for a single parent?
      the cost range *school-age*   Safe   *income*
                                      vs.   single source income
                                   educations → what % of single parents
                                               access financial aid for
                                               child care compared to

7. Counseling style

8. Asian-American students and positive stereotypes

9. The charter school movement in the twentieth century

10. Diet and exercise

hyp - think will be answer.   r.q. - question!

Activity 2.3:
Operational Definitions

Which of the following are operational definitions for the phrase "motivated to learn in a research methods class" and why?

1. Smiles a lot in class.

2. Is observed by the teacher asking questions about past and present reading assignments.

3. Tells the instructor s/he would rather conduct a literature review than interview students.

4. States s/he likes the instructor.

5. Is described by the instructor as a student who hands in all assignments on time.

6. Has a record of checking out books on research design at the library.

7. Enjoys reading journal articles on quasi-experimental studies.

8. Scored 100 percent on the midterm exam.

9. Asks the instructor if s/he can prepare an extra-credit assignment on recent trends in the field of educational research.

10. Voluntarily creates an interactive Web site for the class so that students can discuss course material online.

Activity 2.4:
Justification

A researcher wished to study the following question: "Are 'open' classrooms more effective (do children learn more) than structured, non-open classrooms?"

Here are two different justifications that were written. Which do you think would be most likely to convince skeptics of the importance of the study?

(1) The general purpose of this research is to add knowledge to the field of education at this time when classroom freedom is a cornerstone of today's educational revolution. Various authorities (Leonard, Holt, Kozel, etc.) have suggested that the strictly structured, teacher-directed classroom may impede the learning process of students. They argue that less-structured, "open" environments may help students to learn more, faster, and in greater depth. It is this controversial thesis (since many "structuralists" disagree strongly) that has provoked many teachers to modify their classrooms in hopes of achieving greater educational gains for their students. While the reformers have written convincingly from an inspirational point of view, scant "hard data" exists to provide support. If educators are to jump on this bandwagon, and if money is to be diverted from the more traditional type of arrangement to support open classrooms, they should have information of the type that answers to this research question will provide. It is one thing to think something has potential for improving the learning of the young; it is quite another to have evidence that illustrates that this is so. Hopefully, this study will provide some information in this regard.

(2) Education of children in elementary schools has always been a controversial issue among parents and teachers. There are various ideas regarding the type of setting that would be (or provides) a constructive learning situation for children. One such setting might be the open classroom type. That is what this research will set out to determine.

Activity 2.5:
Evaluating Research Questions

In this activity, you will interview another student in your class about their research question. Evaluate his or her question with regard to each of the following characteristics of good research questions that we presented in Chapter Two in the text.

1.   The question is *feasible*.

_____ **Yes,** the question can be investigated without a considerable amount of time, energy, or money.

_____ **No**, as stated, it would take a considerable amount of time, energy, or money to investigate this question.

Suggestions for improvement _____

2.   The question is *clear*.

_____ **Yes**, most people <u>would</u> agree as to what each of the key words in the question mean.

_____ **No,** most people <u>would not</u> agree as to what each of the key words in the question mean

Suggestions for improvement _____

3.   The question is <u>*significant.*</u>

_____ **Yes,** this question is worth investigating because it will contribute important knowledge about the human condition.

_____ **No,** answers to this question <u>would not</u> contribute important knowledge about the human condition.

Suggestions for improvement _____

4.   The question is *ethical*.

_____ **Yes,** the question will not involve physical or psychological harm or damage to human beings, or to the natural or social environment.

_____ **No,** the question could involve physical or psychological harm or damage to human beings, or to the natural or social environment.

Suggestions for improvement _____

5.   The question suggests a _relationship_.

_____ **Yes,** the question <u>does</u> suggest a relationship of some sort.

_____ **No,** the question <u>does not</u> suggest a relationship.

Suggestions for improvement _____

14

CHAPTER 3: Variables and Hypotheses

Activity 3.1:
Directional vs. Non-Directional Hypotheses

For each of the hypotheses listed below, indicate in the space provided whether it is directional (D) or non-directional (ND).

1. _____ Students taught by a team of three teachers will like the subject taught more than will students taught by one teacher.

2. _____ Male and female elementary school teachers will differ in the amount of satisfaction they receive from teaching.

3. _____ Students who engage in higher levels of gross physical activity will have lower achievement levels, while students who engage in lower levels of gross physical activity will have higher achievement levels.

4. _____ Patients receiving drug "A" will, on average, have fewer heart attacks than patients receiving drug "B."

5. _____ First-, second-, and third-graders will feel differently toward school.

measure an activity more evaluly than survey results.

① Prof who recieve higher ratings from students spend more than 2 hrs a week in office hours.

③ There are no women CEO's in fortune 500 companies.

Activity 3.2:
Testing Hypotheses

Most people have ideas that could be researched if they wished to investigate the ideas more carefully. These ideas usually come from one or more *observations*; that is, from noticing events and how they are related to other events. Here are some examples:

1. The best professors at the university are really interested in their students.

   how do you measure it?

2. Parents who order their kids not to use drugs are more likely to have kids who try drugs than those who let their kids make their own decisions about whether or not to use drugs.

3. Women don't get appointed to top management positions in industry.

   Each of the above statements is an observation about a relationship between two factors. Identify the two factors for which a relationship is implied in each statement and write them in the spaces provided below.

1. *goodness* ~~Best professors~~ is related to *degree of intrest in students*

   authoritative
2. *Parental dictatorship* *style* is related to *drug use in children*

3. *gender* is related to *management promotion*

   Notice that these are assertions. They are not necessarily true. They are at the very least a person's subjective impressions. Restate each below in such a way that we could test them — that is, check them out to see if the statements are true.

1. *When an If* *perceptions of their prof. that they are* ~~If drop~~ *students are intrested in them as* *relates to quality of teaching* *indicated by a survey, then end-of the year* *surveys will indicate that students have*

① *If quality of professors is related to* *degree of* *intrest in students, then*

② *If a dictative parental style relates to drug use in children, then more children of controling parents will use drugs.*

③ *If gender is related to management, then women will not have as many* ~~top management positions~~ *as men. Department Head Positions as men.*

Activity 3.3:
Categorical vs. Quantitative Variables

For each of the variables listed below, indicate whether it is categorical (CV), or quantitative (QV).

1. _____ Counseling style (Rogerian vs. non-Rogerian)

2. _____ Scores on a ten-point biology quiz

3. _____ Grade level (freshman, sophomore, junior, senior)

4. _____ Handedness (left- vs. right-handed)

5. _____ Weight (in pounds)

6. _____ Religion (Buddhist, Catholic, Jewish, Protestant, Other)

7. _____ Grade point average

8. _____ Anxiety level

Activity 3.4:
Independent and Dependent Variables

For each of the situations listed below, name the independent and the dependent variable. Also identify the constant if there is one.

1. Half of a group of third-graders was shown a film on "sharing," while the other half was not shown the film. The attitudes of the students in both groups toward sharing candy was then measured, and their average scores were compared.

The independent variable is _groups of students_

The dependent variable is _attitude toward sharing_

The constant is _age, all given candy_

2. A U.S. history class of eleventh-grade students was randomly divided into three groups. One group was taught a unit on the Civil War using a standard textbook; the second group was taught the same unit using a series of case studies in addition to the textbook; and the third group was taught using the textbook, the case studies, and some audiovisual materials. Student knowledge about the events of the Civil War was compared at the end of the unit.

The independent variable is _method /materials_

The dependent variable is _student knowledge_

The constant is _age, content_

3. Fourteen elementary schools in a large urban school district were selected to participate in a study investigating the effects of computers on learning. Seven of the schools, chosen at random, received new Macintosh computers for every student in their fifth/sixth-grade classes to use, while the other seven did not receive or possess any computers. At the end of the semester, student achievement in the two groups of schools was compared.

The independent variable is _having computers or not_

The dependent variable is _student achievement_

The constant is _same district, age._

Activity 3.5:
Formulating a Hypothesis

In this activity, you will pair off with another student in the class to review each other's research question at this point, and see if it lends itself to a hypothesis.

1. As I understand it, my partner intends to investigate the following question:

   _____
   _____
   _____

2. Restated as a hypothesis, it looks like (or could look like) this:

   _____
   _____
   _____

3. Here are my questions and/or concerns at this point:

   _____
   _____
   _____

Activity 3.6:
Moderator Variables

In this activity, you will work with a partner to not only identify the independent and dependent variables in each of the following hypotheses, but also see if you can add an appropriate moderator variable to each.

1. Students taught by the case-study method will learn more chemistry that students taught by the lecture method.

    The independent variable is _____

    The dependent variable is _____

    A possible moderator variable is _____

2. Students whose parents participate with them in school-related activities are more likely to do well in school than students whose parents do not participate.

    The independent variable is _____

    The dependent variable is _____

    A possible moderator variable is _____

3. The amount of time students spend studying is directly related to the grades they receive.

    The independent variable is _____

    The dependent variable is _____

    A possible moderator variable is _____

4. Learning-disabled children who receive individualized instruction will show greater progress in intellectual development over a year's time than learning-disable children who are taught in groups.

    The independent variable is _____

    The dependent variable is _____

    A possible moderator variable is _____

5.   Eighth graders are more likely to have a stronger preference for works of fiction than for works of non-fiction.

The independent variable is _____

The dependent variable is _____

A possible moderator variable is _____

CHAPTER 4: Ethics and Research

Activity 4.1:
Ethical or not?

In this activity, you are to pair up with another student to discuss each of the following. Then report your conclusions to the class.

1. A professional sex therapist in a large Midwestern city is interested in obtaining more information about the sexual preferences of both heterosexual and homosexual men. He designs a questionnaire that includes a number of highly personal questions and asks a professor at a nearby university to administer it to the students in her introductory psychology class. All of the students in the class are required to complete the questionnaire. Is there an ethical problem here?

2. The spread of AIDS (acquired immune-deficiency syndrome) has brought about a considerable amount of research into the effectiveness of various drugs that control the disease. The U.S. Food and Drug Administration restricted the distribution of these drugs until they were clinically tested. During the tests, some AIDS patients would receive these drugs (the experimental group) while others (the control group would not. Some members of the control group even received a placebo. AIDS patients strongly objected, saying this was unethical. Were they justified in doing so? Why or why not? Is there an ethical dilemma here?

3. In the summer of 1972, newspapers around the country revealed that for 40 years the U.S. Public Health Service (PHS) had been conducting a study to investigate the effects of untreated syphilis on black males in Macon County, Alabama. Public Health Service physicians had administered a variety of blood tests and regular examinations to 399 men who were in various stages of the disease and to 200 others who were in a control group. The study was limited strictly to compiling data on the effects of syphilis and not on ways to treat the disease.

    The participants were never told the purpose of the study or for what they were or were not being treated. No drugs were ever used with these men. A PHS nurse who was monitoring the participants informed local physicians as to who was participating in the study and informed them that they were not to be treated for syphilis. In fact, some of the participants who were offered treatment by other physicians were told they would be dropped from the study if they took the treatment.

    The participants were never aware of the danger to which they were exposed by the study. Furthermore, no effort was ever made to explain their situation to them. In fact, they were enticed with a variety of incentives to participate, such as hot meals, free treatment for other ailments, free rides to and from the clinic, even a $50 burial stipend.

    What ethical standards were violated in this study?

Activity 4.2:
Some Ethical Dilemmas

1. A psychologist conducts the following experiment: A team of subjects plays a game of skill against a computer for money rewards. Unknown to the subjects, one team member is a stooge whose stupidity causes the team to lose regularly. The experimenter observes the subjects through one-way glass. Her intent is to study the behavior of the subjects toward the "stupid" team member.

       This experiment involves no risk to the subjects and is intended simply to create the kind of situation that might occur in any pickup basketball game. To create the situation, the subjects are deceived. Is this deception morally objectionable? Explain your position.

2. Almost all clinical trials that have studied the effects of such factors as blood cholesterol, taking aspirin, or exercise on heart attacks have used middle-aged male subjects. Women's groups have complained that this leads to better health information about men that about women. The researchers reply that in order to get clear results in the five years or so that such a study lasts, they must choose their subjects from the groups that are most likely to have heart attacks. That points to middle-aged men. What would you suggest?

3. The information given to potential subjects in a clinical trial before asking them to decide whether or not to participate might include:

    a. The basic statement that an experiment is being conducted; that is, something beyond simply treating your medical problem will occur in your therapy.
    b. A statement of any potential risks from any of the experimental treatments.
    c. An explanation that a coin will be tossed to decide which treatment you get.
    d. An explanation that one "treatment" is a placebo and a statement of the probability that you will receive the placebo.

Do you feel that all of this information is ethically required? Discuss.

Activity 4.3:
Violations of Ethical Practice

Listed below in Column A are a number of violations of ethical practice. Match the letter of the violation from Column B with the example listed in Column A to which the violation refers.

Column A: Practice	Column B: Ethical violation
1. _____ Researcher requires a group of high school sophomores to sign a form in which they agree to participate in a research study.	a. Protecting participants from harm.
	b. Ensuring confidentiality of research data.
2. _____ Researcher asks first-graders sensitive questions without obtaining the consent of their parents to question them.	c. Deception of subjects.
3. _____ Researcher deletes data he collects that does not support his hypothesis.	d. Right of an individual to participate or withdraw from a study at any time.
4. _____ Researcher gives information to students to see whether it increases their stress when taking an examination.	e. Reporting accurately the results of a research investigation.
5. _____The teachers in a study of punitive practices are told that it is their students who are being observed.	f. Coercion of subjects.
	g. Parental permission.

Activity 4.4:
Why Would These Research Practices Be Unethical?

Figure 4.2 in Chapter Four in the text presents a number of individuals describing unethical research practices. Working with a partner, in the space provided below, explain why each of the statements suggests something that would be unethical.

1. "We are required to ask you to sign this consent form. You needn't read it; it's just routine."

   _____

   _____

   _____

2. "A few cases seemed quite different from the rest, so we deleted them"

   _____

   _____

   _____

3. "Yes, as a student at this university you are required to participate in this study."

   _____

   _____

   _____

4. "There is no need to tell any of the parents that we are modifying the school lunch diet for this study."

   _____

   _____

   _____

5. "Requiring students to participate in class discussions might be harmful to some, but it is necessary for our research."

   _____

   _____

   _____

Activity 4.5:
Is It Ethical to Use Prisoners as Subjects?

1. Discuss the following question: What might be some arguments for and against using prison inmates as the subjects in a research study?

Argument For	Argument Against

CHAPTER 5: Locating and Reviewing the Literature

Activity 5.1: Library Worksheet

Activity 5.2: Where Would You Look?

Activity 5.3: Do a Computer Search of the Literature

Activity 5.1:
Library Worksheet

LOCATIONS FOR LIBRARY SOURCE MATERIAL

Be sure you can locate each of the following

1. *Education Index*   Location: _____

2. *Journal of Educational Research*   Location: _____

3. NSSE Yearbooks   Location: _____

4. *Encyclopedia of Educational Research*   Location: _____

5. M.A. theses   Location: _____

6. *Dissertation Abstracts International* (DAI)   Location: _____

7. The research journal in your field   Location: _____

8. *ERIC*   Location: _____

9. The World Wide Web   Location: _____

What is the name of the major journal(s) in your field?

_____

_____

_____

Activity 5.2:
Where Would You Look?

Where might you look to find information about each of the following?

1. A review of recent research on moral education

2. A brief summary of the history of educational programs for the gifted

3. A topic of interest that has not been reviewed during the last two years

4. A summary of a recently published article in the field of psychology

5. A summary of a Ph.D. dissertation on mastery learning

6. An article published within the last month on social studies education

7. Some of the major ideas in educational sociology

8. Some popular articles on education that appeared during the last year in *U.S. News and World Report* and *Newsweek* magazines

Activity 5.3:
Do a Computer Search of the Literature

Use ERIC to do a computer search of the literature on a topic of interest to you.

1. The topic I chose for my search was (describe as precisely as you can below):

_____

_____

_____

2. I reviewed _____ (number) of references.

3. I used the following descriptors:

_____

_____

_____

4. Here are the results of my search.

Search #1 _____

Search #2 _____

Search #3 _____

Search #4 _____

5. Here are the names of three of the references (abstracts or articles) identified using these descriptors.

_____

_____

_____

CHAPTER 6: Sampling

Activity 6.1:
Identifying Types of Sampling

For each of the situations described below, identify the type of sampling that is being used.

a. Simple random sampling
b. Stratified random sampling
c. Cluster sampling
d. Two-stage random sampling

e. Convenience sampling
f. Purposive sampling
g. No sampling -- entire population is being studied

1. _____ A researcher surveying options about a university president first determines the proportion of the total faculty in each college in the university. She then randomly selects the same proportions for her sample.

2. _____ A researcher is interested in interviewing all the members of the New York City police force who do not live in the city. He gets a roster of the names of all officers on the force, randomly selects five police stations, and then conducts interviews of all officers in those stations.

3. _____ A researcher is interested interviewing alumni of San Simeon College who graduated between the years 1990 and 1996. He gets the roster of the names of these individuals from the alumni office, and mails a questionnaire to everyone on this roster.

4. _____ Another researcher is also interested in interviewing alumni of San Simeon College who graduated between the years 1990 and 1996. He gets the roster of the names of these individuals from the alumni office, selects the names of 100 individuals who graduated during these years using a table of random numbers, and then mails a questionnaire to everyone selected.

5. _____ A researcher is interested in identifying the attitudes of the physicians who work for Keyser Hospital toward the Republican plan for health care. She obtains a list of all the Keyser Medical Centers in southern California and randomly selects ten of these centers. Then she obtains a list of all the physicians at these centers and randomly selects eight physicians from each center to interview.

6. _____ A graduate student enrolled in the Marriage and Family Counseling Program at Daytona University is interested in determining how other graduate students feel about the program. He interviews all of the students he has access to on a given Monday night when he takes one of his counseling courses.

7. _____ A student enrolled in the Hotel and Restaurant Management School at Colorado State is researching the best restaurants in Denver based on the opinions of food critics. She begins by asking her advisor, who refers the student to four food critics who have written extensively on the subject and whom the student then contacts to interview for her study.

8. _____Fifty black marbles are selected (using a volunteer) from a large jar in which there are 250 marbles, evenly divided between black and white in color.

9. _____A high school teacher interviews all of the students who are members of the school glee club.

10. _____A researcher interviews all the students who are assigned to after-school detention the day before a championship football game.

Activity 6.2:
Drawing a Random Sample

In this exercise, you will use a Table of Random Numbers to draw a random sample, and how the size of a sample affects its representativeness. Use the hypothetical population of 99 students on page 35. Use the Table of Random Numbers located in the back of the textbook to select a sample of 10 students from the hypothetical population. List their numbers in the first column of the chart below, and then fill in the related information from the table on page 35 for each of the students you have selected.

Student Number	Gender	School	IQ

Now, compute the proportion for Gender and School (divide your totals by 10 to obtain a decimal), and the average IQ (divide by 10 to obtain a whole number) for your sample, and enter these into the appropriate boxes below.

Averages Sample (n = 10)	Gender M	F	School A	B	C	IQ
Average =						

Find three other groups or students in the class, obtain the averages they got from their samples on the three characteristics, and write them in the boxes below.

Averages from 3 other groups	Gender M	F	School A	B	C	IQ
Group #1						
Group #2						
Group #3						

Now average the four samples (yours plus the three others), and write the averages in the boxes below.

Averages for Sample (n = 40)	Gender M	F	School A	B	C	IQ
Average =						
Population						

How do the data for the sample of size 10 differ from the data for the sample of size 40? How would you explain this? What conclusion can you draw from this exercise?

_____
_____
_____
_____
_____
_____

Table for Activity 6.2
A Hypothetical Population of 99 Students

Student Number	Sex	School	IQ	Student Number	Sex	School	IQ
01	F	Adams	134	51	M	Beals	110
02	F	Adams	133	52	M	Beals	110
03	F	Adams	130	53	M	Beals	109
04	F	Adams	127	54	M	Beals	108
05	F	Adams	123	55	M	Beals	107
06	M	Adams	123	56	M	Beals	106
07	M	Adams	121	57	M	Beals	101
08	M	Adams	120	58	M	Beals	101
09	F	Adams	119	59	M	Beals	98
10	M	Adams	118	60	M	Beals	97
11	F	Adams	117	61	F	Beals	91
12	F	Adams	117	62	F	Beals	86
13	M	Adams	115	63	F	Beals	83
14	M	Adams	111	64	F	Cortez	137
15	M	Adams	109	65	M	Cortez	136
16	M	Adams	108	66	F	Cortez	133
17	M	Adams	108	67	F	Cortez	130
18	F	Adams	106	68	F	Cortez	128
19	F	Adams	105	69	F	Cortez	125
20	F	Adams	104	70	F	Cortez	125
21	F	Adams	103	71	M	Cortez	122
22	F	Adams	101	72	F	Cortez	121
23	F	Adams	101	73	M	Cortez	118
24	M	Adams	101	74	F	Cortez	118
25	M	Adams	100	75	M	Cortez	113
26	M	Adams	98	76	F	Cortez	113
27	M	Adams	97	77	M	Cortez	111
28	M	Adams	97	78	F	Cortez	111
29	M	Adams	96	79	F	Cortez	107
30	F	Adams	95	80	F	Cortez	106
31	F	Adams	89	81	F	Cortez	106
32	F	Adams	88	82	F	Cortez	105
33	F	Adams	85	83	F	Cortez	104
34	F	Beals	133	84	F	Cortez	103
35	F	Beals	129	85	F	Cortez	102
36	F	Beals	129	86	M	Cortez	102
37	F	Beals	128	87	M	Cortez	100
38	F	Beals	127	88	M	Cortez	100
39	F	Beals	127	89	M	Cortez	99
40	F	Beals	126	90	M	Cortez	99
41	M	Beals	125	91	M	Cortez	99
42	M	Beals	124	92	F	Cortez	98
43	M	Beals	117	93	M	Cortez	97
44	M	Beals	116	94	F	Cortez	96
45	M	Beals	115	95	F	Cortez	95
46	M	Beals	114	96	F	Cortez	93
47	M	Beals	114	97	F	Cortez	85
48	M	Beals	113	98	M	Cortez	83
49	M	Beals	111	99	M	Cortez	83
50	M	Beals	111				

Parameters: Average IQ = 109.8; Proportions: sex: M = .49, F = .51; schools: A = .33, B = .31, C = .36

Activity 6.3:
When Is It Appropriate to Generalize?

1. On a television talk show, a psychiatrist discussed his study of airplane hijackers at some length and pointed out that their outstanding characteristic (which he discovered through extensive psychiatric interviewing) was a consistent history of failure. His sample consisted of approximately 20 hijackers who were interviewed while in jail. Although not explicitly stated, it seems obvious that the population to whom he intended to generalize was "all hijackers." Would it be appropriate to generalize to this population?

   Yes _____   No __X__   If not, why not?

   not enough data about population

   _____

2. Assume that you wish to study the hypothesis that among career women between the ages of 30 and 50, career satisfaction is related to the adequacy of their relationship with their father during adolescence. Work with a partner to answer each of the following questions.

a. What target population would you want to generalize? _women between_ _30-50 with careers_

   _____

b. What population would be sufficiently accessible? _~~State~~ Cumberland county_ _female dominated professions?_

   _____

c. How might you get a random sample from the accessible population? _____

   Cluster sampling - assess buisness - randomly sample.

   _____

d. If you had to use a convenience sample -- for example, in just one or two locations, -- what descriptive information should you try to obtain?

   range _Qual. - pay - benefits_
   age, job, Sat, -hrs

   _____

Activity 6.4:
True or False?

Write "T" in front of the statements below that are true; write "F" in front of those that are false.

1. _____ A "population," as used in research, refers to the group to whom the researcher wishes to generalize the results of a study.

2. _____ Systematic sampling would be an example of a random sampling method.

3. _____ A purposive sample is a sample selected because the individuals have special characteristics or qualities of some sort.

4. _____ A representative sample is one that is similar to its population in all characteristics.

5. _____ The target population is usually larger than the accessible population.

6. _____ A simple random sample is usually a convenience sample.

7. _____ When a study is replicated, it is not always repeated under the same conditions.

8. _____ The term "ecological generalizability" refers to the extent to which the results of a study can be generalized to conditions or settings different from those that existed in a particular study.

9. _____ The term "external validity," as used in research, refers to whether the sample has been randomly selected or not.

10. _____ Convenience samples can be randomly selected.

Activity 6.5:
Stratified Sampling

In this activity, you will use a table of random numbers to select a stratified random sample.

A hypothetical school district includes a total of 35 administrators. Their last names are shown in the table below. Their school level is indicated by the letters E (elementary) and S (secondary). You are authorized to send eight of the District's administrators to a professional conference. Use a table of random numbers to choose a stratified random sample to determine who gets to go. You want the sample to be as representative as possible of the administrators in the district.

Gordon Abel - E	Mary Smith - S	Louise Chan - E	Don Green - E	Susan Thomas – E
Danny Gordon - E	Faye Taam - E	Tony Gomez - S	Tom Vilueva - S	Ed Peregrino – E
Phyllis Guta - E	Joan Miller - S	Ed Lopez - E	Peter Potter - E	James Turk – E
Joan Nunez - E	Dottie Arnot - E	Bernie Beber - S	Ruth Cho - E	Mike Fujimoto – E
Paul Lichter - E	Susan Focht - E	Betty Davis - E	Sue Kowoski - E	Stan Leung – E
Alice Astor - S	Jane Dunlap - E	Rob Roberts - E	Annie Lai - E	Jesus Contras – E
Barbara Derek - E	Bob Wagus - E	Tyrone Power - S	Sally Bender - S	Dick Cross – S

a. What are the strata you will use?

b. Write down the names of the eight individuals you have selected.

c. Explain how you selected the eight.

d. How representative is your sample? Explain why it is or is not.

Would there be a better way to determine who should attend this meeting? If not, explain why this is the best method to use. If so, describe how you would select a better, more representative sample.

Activity 6.6:
Designing a Sampling Plan

In this activity, you will work with a partner to develop a sampling plan.

Suppose that you would like to select a sample of 50 students at your school to learn something about how many hours per week, on average, students in your program spend engaged in studying.

a. Discuss with your partner whether you think it would be easy or difficult to obtain a simple random sample of students and to obtain the desired information from all students selected for the sample. Summarize your discussion by writing a few sentences (to read to the class) explaining why you think it would be easy or difficult.

b. With your partner, decide how you might go about selecting a sample of 50 students from your school that, although it truly may not be a simple random sample, could be reasonably considered representative of the population of interest. Write a brief description of your sampling plan, and be sure to point out the aspects of the plan that you think make it reasonable to argue that it will be representative.

c. Explain your plan to another pair of students in the class. Ask them to critique the plan, pointing out any potential flaws they see in it. Write a brief summary of the comments you received. Now reverse roles and provide a critique of their sampling plan.

d. Based on the feedback you just received, would you modify your original sampling plan? If not, explain why this is not necessary. If so, describe how the plan would be modified.

CHAPTER 7: Instrumentation

Activity 7.1:
Major Categories of Instruments and Their Uses

Match the letter of the instrument from Column B with its most likely use listed in Column A.

Column A: Purpose	Column B: Instrument
1. _____ A researcher wishes to observe and record the behavior of an individual over time.	a. Questionnaire
2. _____ A researcher wishes to survey a large group of individuals.	b. Interview schedule
	c. Performance checklist
3. _____ A researcher wants to find out how much someone knows about the causes of the French Revolution.	d. Achievement test
	e. Attitude scale
4. _____A researcher wants to evaluate the quality of a new microwave oven.	f. Rating scale
	g. Anecdotal record
5. _____A researcher wishes to get in-depth information from a small group of people.	
6. _____ A researcher wants to gain some idea of how students in a graduate program in teacher education feel about their student teaching experience.	

Activity 7.2:
Which Type of Instrument is Most Appropriate?

For each of the items listed below, indicate whether it would be most likely to be measured by an aptitude test (AT), a questionnaire (Q), an interview (I), a rating scale (RS), a tally sheet (TS), or a performance checklist (PC).

Q 1. *RS* _____ a person's self-concept or *I*

2. *PC* _____ readiness for kindergarten or *AT*

3. *I* _____ a person's experiences in high school or *Q*

4. *PC* _____ assessing paramedic skills

5. *RS* _____ quality of a college application

6. *Q* _____ ability to work with others on a research project or *AT or RS or TS*

7. *I* _____ educational experiences of exceptional teachers   or *Q*

8. *AT* _____ potential of high school seniors for college work   or *RS or PC or I*

9. *TS* _____ type of questions asked by students in a chemistry class

10. *TS* _____ prevalence of different kinds of errors in baseball

RS 11. *Q* _____ student evaluations of instructor competence

12. *I* _____ how a particular student feels about poetry

13. *Q* _____ public reactions to a recently announced plan to raise property taxes

14. *PC* _____ ability to use a calculator

15. *TS* _____ who participates -- and how much -- in the discussions that occur in an advanced-placement twelfth-grade American government class

Activity 7.3:
Types of Scales

Match the letter of the type of measurement scale from Column B with the example listed in Column A to which the scale applies.

Column A: Practice	Column B: Measurement Scale
1. _____ Type of scale that possesses a true zero point	a. Nominal scale
2. _____ Type of scale that possesses all of the characteristics of the other scales	b. Ordinal scale
3. _____ Type of scale that indicates only relative standing among individuals	c. Interval scale
4. _____ Type of scale in which a researcher simply assigns numbers to different categories in order to show differences	d. Ratio scale
5. _____ Type of scale that is rarely encountered in educational research	
6. _____ Type of scale that cannot be used to measure quantitative variables	
7. _____ Type of scale in which all of the distances between the points on the scale are equal, but does not have a true zero point	
8. _____ The simplest type of scale that provides the least information	
9. _____ Type of scale that assumes that equal differences between scores really mean equal differences in the variable being measured	

Activity 7.4:
Norm-Referenced vs. Criterion-Referenced Instruments

For each of the items listed below, indicate whether Norm-referenced (N) or Criterion-referenced (C) instrument is described.

1. _____ Provides a clear-cut goal to work toward

2. _____ Indicates that an individual was able to run a mile in at least 12 minutes

3. _____ Compares an individual's scores with the scores of a group

4. _____ Focuses more directly on instruction than the other type

5. _____ Indicates how an individual did compared to other members in his or her class

6. _____ Is almost always easier to use than the other type

7. _____ Desired difficulty level is at or about 50 percent

8. _____ Generally is inferior than the other type for research purposes

9. _____ Generally will provide more variability in scores

Activity 7.5:
Developing a Rating Scale

In one of our research classes, a student designed a study to investigate the following hypothesis:

"The more open the classroom, the higher the amount of student motivation."

As part of the process, she developed a rating scale to assess both the degree of openness and the level of student motivation within a particular classroom. Only by having some kind of measurement of each of these variables could she determine if a relationship existed between them.

Her first step was to produce a number of items related to the idea of "openness." She began by listing various things that could be taken as indicators of openness. Certain groupings began to emerge from the list of indicators. For example, a number of indicators seemed to concern the physical arrangement of the classroom, so that constituted one grouping. Listed below are some of the indicators and categories she formulated:

Physical environment: Are the desks placed in rows? Are there specific learning centers for subjects? Are classes sometimes held outdoors? Is there a general meeting area for students in the classroom? Are any other types of furniture used besides desks (e.g., sofas, rocking chairs, etc.) used? How many adults (teaches, paraprofessionals, etc.) are there in the classroom?

Curriculum: What amount of time does the teacher spend on planning? On evaluation? Does the teacher have a list of overall objectives she tries to attain? How much time is spent on the academic curriculum? On arts and crafts? On discussions or problem solving? Do the students direct their own planning? Devise their own curriculum? Are affective objectives included in the curriculum? Are students taught to express their feelings? Are grades given?

Teacher-student relationships: How often does the teacher give directions? Help students? How often do students initiate activities? Can students leave the classroom on their own, or must they request permission? Does the teacher work with students individually? Work in small groups? Teach the entire class? Do students and teachers jointly evaluate student work? Are class meetings student or teacher-directed? Can students set their own free time?

Materials: Are students assigned specific materials to use? What kinds of materials are available to students? How much time is spent on workbook assignments? Are there manipulative materials available? Are the materials easily accessible, or must students request them? Is the use of materials directed by teacher or students? Are art materials available? What sorts of books do students use? What other materials exist?

Social environment: Are students encouraged to help one another? To tutor others? Are students free to talk with others in class? How often? Do students work alone, or may they work with others? Do students group themselves, or is this done by the teacher? Do students share in room cleanup? How many times must the teacher ask for quiet? Does physical aggression ever occur between students? If so, how often? Who handles aggression, teacher or students?

Parental participation: Are parents allowed in the classroom? Observers? Others? Are parents and others free to enter the classroom when they wish, or is there a formal procedure they must go through? Is there a volunteer parent-aide program? What kinds of tasks do parents perform? How often are parents present?

Once she felt that she had a sufficient number of items within each of these categories, she worked to refine and clarify the indicators in each of the categories and then to convert them into items for a rating scale. Shown below is her completed rating scale:

RATING SCALE FOR CLASSROOM OPENNESS

1. Students do not move without teacher permission	1 2 3 4 5	1. Students may move in or out of class without permission
2. All students work at the same task at the same time	1 2 3 4 5	2. A great variety of tasks are performed at the same time
3. The teacher is the only resource in the classroom	1 2 3 4 5	3. Several human resources other than the teacher are in the Classroom
4. Human resources are only clerical or housekeeper aides to the teacher	1 2 3 4 5	4. Human resources interact with students or with small groups
5. Furniture is permanently arranged	1 2 3 4 5	5. Furniture is spontaneously arranged
6. Everyone works at own desk	1 2 3 4 5	6. There are many floating study centers
7. Desks, tables, and chairs are arranged traditionally	1 2 3 4 5	7. There is a complete variety of furniture in a variety of arrangements
8. Students cannot interact without direct permission of the teacher	1 2 3 4 5	8. Students are free to interact with others in any way they desire
9. The teacher initiates all the activities	1 2 3 4 5	9. Students also initiate activities
10. The teacher teaches the class as a group	1 2 3 4 5	10. The teacher works with small groups or individual students

11. The teacher is addressed formally (e.g., Mrs. X; hands are raised; etc.)	1 2 3 4 5	11. The teacher is addressed informally (first name, etc.)
12. Reprimands are punitive	1 2 3 4 5	12. No reprimands or only friendly reminders are given
13. No feelings are verbally	1 2 3 4 5	13. Feelings are expressed verbally
14. The textbook is closely followed	1 2 3 4 5	14. No formally prepared materials are used in class

What differences do you notice between the original list of indicators and the final rating scale above?

_____

_____

_____

_____

_____

_____

_____

Activity 7.6:
Design an Instrument

In this activity, you are to design an instrument (see Chapter 7 in the text) on a topic of interest.

1. Prepare either a rating scale or a questionnaire and describe it on the back of this page.

2. In the spaces below, describe how you checked for:

instrument validity _____

_____

_____

instrument reliability _____

_____

_____

3. Administer the instrument to a group (at least five) of your friends. Summarize the results here. _____

_____

_____

_____

_____

4. What problems did you encounter? _____

_____

_____

5. What could you do better next time to avoid such problems? _____

_____

_____

CHAPTER 8: Validity and Reliability

Activity 8.1:
Instrument Validity

A valid instrument is one that measures what it says it measures. If a researcher is interested in measuring how much a student knows about the U.S. Civil War, for example, he or she needs an instrument that will measure exactly that -- the student's knowledge -- *not* his or her feelings, attitudes, beliefs, or skills. For each of the two objectives listed below, write one example of the kind of question or observation you might engage in to measure, at least to some extent, attainment of the objective.

1. **Objective:** To measure the degree to which a person enjoys modern art

Instrument question or observation strategy:

Survey—rate scale

interview —

2. **Objective**: To measure the level of anxiety that exists among university students during final exam period

Instrument question or observation strategy:

physical examination
Survey - scale
interview —

3. **Objective**: To measure the attitudes of local residents toward the building of a new ballpark in downtown San Francisco

Instrument question or observation strategy:

Activity 8.2:
Instrument Reliability (1)

A *reliable* instrument is one that is *consistent* in what it measures. If an individual scores highly on the first administration of a test, for example, he or she should, if the test is reliable, score highly on a second administration. In this activity, you are going to evaluate the reliability of an instrument.

Imagine that you are conducting a study for which you must develop a mastery test in mathematics for ninth-grade students. You develop a 30-point test and distribute it to a class of 13 ninth-graders in a certain school district on the west coast of the United States in May of 2004. You then give the test again one month later to the day in June, 2004. The scores of the students on the two administrations of the test are shown below. Plot each pair of scores on the scatterplot started below. We have entered "A's" scores to get you started. What do they suggest to you about the reliability of this? Explain.

	30-POINT MATHEMATICS MASTERY TEST (FIRST ADMINISTRATION)	30-POINT MATHEMATICS MASTERY TEST (SECOND ADMINISTRATION)
A	17	15
B	22	18
C	25	21
D	12	15
E	7	14
F	28	27
G	27	24
H	8	5
I	21	25
J	24	21
K	27	27
L	21	19
M	10	15

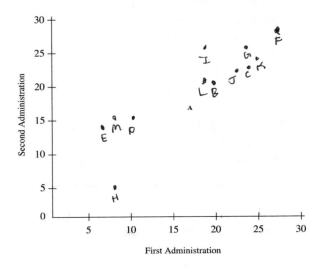

First Administration

Activity 8.3:
Instrument Reliability (2)

For each of the situations listed below, match the type of reliability with what the researchers involved are evaluating.

Column A: Situation	Column B: Instrument Reliability
1. _____ A researcher develops two versions of a test meant to measure interests in students prior to their taking an examination. He gives one version of the test to a group of college sophomores on a Monday, and the other version of the test to them the next day.	a. internal consistency b. test-retest reliability c. equivalent forms reliability d. none of the above
2. _____ A teacher develops a new test for high school biology. She gives the test twice, once to the students in her morning class and once to the students in her afternoon class. She then compares the scores for the two classes of students.	
3. _____ A college professor is interested in evaluating her end-of-semester course evaluations that are completed by her students. The instrument consists of 20 five-point rating scale items. She obtains an average score for each student on the first 10 items, and also an average score for each student on the second 10 items. She then compares the scores.	
4. _____ A researcher prepares a 15-item multiple-choice test designed to measure student knowledge of the causes of the Spanish-American War. She asks two of her colleagues, specialists in American history, to identify any items that they think do not measure what she is after.	
5. _____ A teacher prepares an algebra test and gives it to her students at the end of the semester and again two months later.	

6. Which of the following would be a way of assessing unreliability due to content and time?

a. Administering a reading test (Form X) on Monday and again one month later
b. Administering a reading test (Form X) on Monday and calculating a split-half correlation
c. Administering a reading test (Form X) on Monday and Form Y one month later
d. Administering a reading test (Form X) on Monday and deleting any questions that more than 50 percent of those taking the test missed

Activity 8.4:
What Kind of Evidence: Content-Related, Criterion-Related or Construct-Related?

As we mention in the text, *validity* depends on the amount and type of evidence there is to support one's interpretations concerning data that has been collected. In Chapter Eight, we describe three kinds of evidence that a researcher might collect: content-related, criterion-related, and construct-related evidence of validity.

Listed below are a number of questions that each represent one of these three types. In the space provided, write *content* if the question refers to content-related evidence, *criterion* if the question related to criterion-related evidence, and *construct* if the question refers to construct-related evidence of validity.

1. How strong is the relationship between student scores obtained using this instrument and their teacher's rating of their ability? _____

2. How adequately do the questions in the instrument represent that which is being measured? _____

3. Do the items that the instrument contains logically get at that which is being measured? _____

4. Are there a variety of different *types* of evidence (e.g., test scores, teacher ratings, correlations, etc.) that all measure this variable? _____

5. How well do the scores obtained using this instrument predict future performance? _____

6. Is the format of the instrument appropriate? _____

Activity 8.5:
What Constitutes Construct-Related Evidence of Validity?

On page 156 of the text, we provide an example of one piece of evidence that could be used to establish construct validity for a pencil and paper test on honesty.

1. In the space provided below, after discussing this with a partner, suggest some *additional* information that a researcher might collect as evidence of honesty in an effort to establish construct validity for the test.

_____

_____

_____

_____

_____

_____

_____

2. *What about interest in the subject of chemistry?* Suppose another researcher wishes to develop a test to measure an individual's interest in chemistry. What sort of information might he or she collect in an attempt to establish construct validity for the test?

_____

_____

_____

_____

_____

_____

_____

CHAPTER 9: Internal Validity

Activity 9.1:
Threats to Internal Validity

Which threat to internal validity exists in each of the situations listed below?

Column A: Situation	Column B: Threat to Internal Validity
1. A researcher wishes to compare changes in achievement motivation of males and females during their high school years. During her study, she discovers that more males than females failed to complete high school.	a. Maturation b. Mortality c. Data collector characteristics d. Location e. Instrumentation f. Regression

b 1. A researcher wishes to compare changes in achievement motivation of males and females during their high school years. During her study, she discovers that more males than females failed to complete high school.

c 2. Two groups of students are compared with regard to their attitude toward a career in the military. Two different recruiting officers administer the same attitude scale to each group. The recruiter who administers the scale to the first group is in uniform; the second recruiter is in civilian clothes.

f 3. Those students who score in the top 2 percent on a biology test have, on average, lower scores the second time they take the test.

e? 4. A researcher wants to measure changes in student attitudes toward their graduate programs at a local university. He finds a questionnaire used by another researcher the previous year that asks most of the questions he wants to ask. To improve it, he changes some of the questions and adds a few more.

comparing 2 groups using different test.

a 5. A researcher observes level of attention in a special program during the month of September and again in May.

place in time! chronology

d 6. A researcher interviews two groups of individuals. One group is interviewed in his classroom; the other group, although asked the same questions, is interviewed in the student union.

Activity 9.2:
What Type of Threat?

Match the letter of the appropriate research methodology from Column B with its topic in Column A.

Column A: Examples	Column B: Type of Threat
1. _h_ The scorers of an examination <u>unconsciously</u> grade the exam papers in such a way that some students receive lower scores than they deserve.	a. Subject characteristics
	b. History
	c. Maturation
2. _g_ The taking of a pretest by students participating in a research study allows them to figure out the nature of this study.	d. Attitude of subjects
	e. Mortality
3. _a_ Two existing groups are compared with respect to their scores on an achievement test.	f. Data collector bias
	g. Testing
4. _b_ A fire drill occurs during the taking of a final examination. Several students complain they did not have enough time to complete the exam.	h. Instrument decay
5. _c_ Change during an intervention is due to just the <u>passing of time rather</u> than the intervention itself.	
6. _d_ The way in which students are ask to participate in a study affects how they perform. _Could be "f" if the collector asked._	

Activity 9.3:
Controlling Threats to Internal Validity

Suggest a way to control each of the following threats to internal validity.

1. Instrument decay _____

_____

2. Subject characteristics _____

_____

3. Loss of subjects (mortality) _____

_____

4. Data collector characteristics _____

_____

5. Location _____

_____

6. Regression _____

_____

7. Implementation _____

_____

8. Attitude of subjects _____

_____

CHAPTER 10: Descriptive Statistics

Activity 10.1:
Construct a Frequency Polygon

For the most complete description of a group of scores, construct a **frequency polygon:** a graphic illustration of all the scores in a group. A comparison of frequency polygons is the most meaningful way to evaluate groups of scores. That is what we will do in this activity.

Suppose that you have obtained the scores for two groups of students on a 30-item test of critical thinking. One group has been taught by the inquiry method, and the other group by the lecture method. On the test, the highest score received by a student in either group was 32, and the lowest score was 3. There are 40 students in each group. The raw scores for each group are listed in Table 10.1A below.

Table 10.1A

Raw scores for Group I (Taught by the Inquiry Method)	Raw scores for Group II (Taught by the Lecture Method)
3, 7, 8, 9, 11, 11, 13, 13, 13, 14, 15, 15, 16, 16, 17, 17, 17, 17, 18, 18, 19, 19, 19, 20, 20, 20, 21, 21, 21, 21, 22, 22, 22, 22, 22, 23, 23, 23, 23, 23, 23, 24 24, 24, 25, 25, 26 26, 26, 26, 26, 27, 27 28, 28, 28, 29, 30, 30, 32	5, 7, 9, 9, 10, 10, 11, 11, 11, 12, 13, 13, 13, 13, 14, 14, 15, 15, 15, 15, 15, 16, 16, 17, 17, 17, 17, 18, 18, 18, 18, 20, 20, 20, 20, 20, 20, 20, 20, 20, 21, 21, 22, 22, 22, 22, 22, 23, 23, 23, 24, 25, 25, 26, 26, 28, 28, 28, 30, 30

Now, follow these steps:

Step 1. Determine the difference between the highest and the lowest score. For the inquiry group, this is $32 - 3 = 29$.

Step 2. Divide this difference by 15 and round to the nearest whole number. In this case, $29 / 15 = 1.93$, which rounds to 2. This number is the size of the intervals to be used in the polygon.

Step 3. Beginning with the lowest score, set up intervals as shown in Table 10.1B. Make one interval schedule for each group.

Table 10.1B

Group I: Taught by the Inquiry Method		Group II: Taught by the Lecture Method	
Score	Frequency	Score	Frequency
31-32	/ _ _	31-32	_ _ _
29-30	/ / /	29-30	_ _ _
27-28	_ _ _	27-28	_ _ _
25-26	_ _ _	25-26	_ _ _
23-24	_ _ _	23-24	_ _ _
21-22	_ _ _	21-22	_ _ _
19-20	_ _ _	19-20	_ _ _
17-18	_ _ _	17-18	_ _ _
15-16	_ _ _	15-16	_ _ _
13-14	_ _ _	13-14	_ _ _
11-12	_ _ _	11-12	_ _ _
9-10	_ _ _	9-10	_ _ _
7-8	_ _ _	7-8	_ _ _
5-6	_ _ _	5-6	_ _ _
3-4	_ _ _	3-4	_ _ _

Step 4. Tally the number of scores in each interval for each group and enter the tally in Table 10.1B under the column entitled "Frequency." W have begun this for the inquiry group, using the data from Table 10.1A. As you can see, there is one score of 31 or 32 and three scores of 29 or 30 in the Inquiry group.

Step 5. Draw a pair of axes as shown in Figure 10.1. Mark off points on the X axis to represent the score intervals. The lowest interval is placed near the Y axis. The distance between the points must be the same. Then mark off points on the Y axis to represent frequencies. These must begin with 0. The highest point is the largest frequency in either group. You should have discovered (by looking at your tallies in Table 10.1B) that the largest frequency in the inquiry group is nine (for scores of 21 or 22 and for 23 or 24).

Step 6. Plot each frequency for each interval for the inquiry group. Place an open (white) dot directly opposite a frequency of 1 on the Y axis and directly above the 3-4 interval on the axis. Place another white dot directly opposite a frequency of 0 on the Y axis and directly above the 5-6 interval on the X axis, and so forth until you have all of the frequencies for the inquiry group entered on the graph. Now plot the frequency (which is zero) for one interval below and one interval above the actual range of scores. This is called *anchoring* the polygon.

Step 7. Connect the points (the white dots) in sequence, being sure not to skip any interval. Notice that the line must touch the X axis at both ends: that is why we plotted zero frequencies at interval 1-2 and interval 33-34.

Step 8. Repeat the above steps for the lecture group, only use closed (black) dots. When you are finished, you will have two frequency polygons on the same graph, showing the comparative performances of the inquiry and lecture groups on the critical thinking test.

Which group, overall, performed better?   Inquiry _____ Lecture _____

How can you tell? _____

_____

FIGURE 10.1

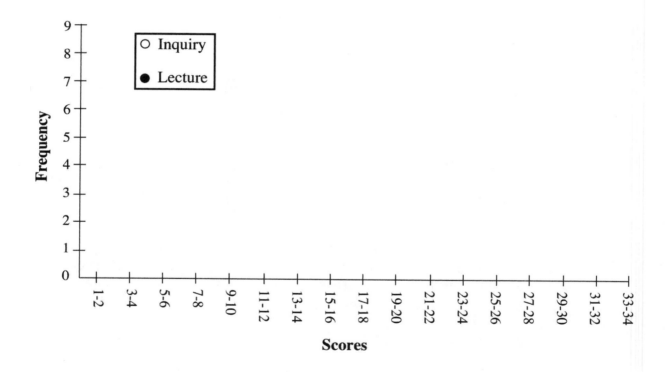

Activity 10.2:
Comparing Frequency Polygons

Often we want to compare two or more groups on some measurement. One way to do this effectively is to use frequency polygons plotted on the same graph. Look at Figure 10.2 below. It illustrates a study in which two fourth-grade classes were compared: one in which a new social studies curriculum was being tried out (E), and a similar comparison group (C). End-of-year scores are being compared, the test being one designed to measure student understanding of social studies concepts.

FIGURE 10.2

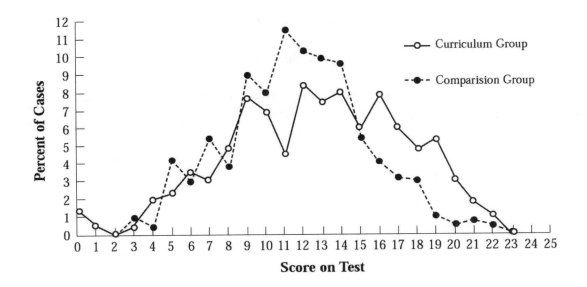

1. What percent of each group received a score of 18 on the test? _____ (E)

   _____ (C)

2. What percent of each group scored above 20? _____ (E)

   _____ (C)

3. The hypothesis for this study was that the curriculum group would outperform the comparison group on the dependent variable. How do the groups compare? Was the hypothesis supported?

   _____

   _____

   _____

Activity 10.3:
Calculating Averages

1. As we discusses in the text, the mean for a group of scores is determined by adding up all of the scores in the group and dividing by the total number of scores in the group. What is the mean for the following group of scores?

    10   12   15   16   20   50

2. The median is the point in a group of scores below and above which 50 percent of the scores fall. What is the median for the group of scores in above?

3. Consider the following two sets of scores:

    Set A: 44, 48, 50, 54, 59

    Set B: 5, 36, 50, 65, 99

How would you describe these two sets of scores? (Hint: Compare their means and medians.) What do these tell you about the two sets?

Activity 10.4:
Calculating the Standard Deviation

Although it takes a bit of time, calculating the standard deviation of a set of scores is actually quite easy. Just follow these steps.

1. List the scores in the first column of a table, as shown in Table 10.2.

2. Calculate the mean of the scores.

3. Subtract the mean from each score to obtain the difference.

4. Square each difference score, as shown in the last column.

5. Sum the scores in the last column.

6. Divide this sum by the total number of scores in the distribution.

7. Take the square root of this number to obtain the standard deviation.

TABLE 10.2

Score	Subtract	Mean	Equals	Difference	Square the Difference
5	-	20	=	-15	225
10	-	20	=	-10	100
15	-	20	=	-5	25
20	-	20	=	0	0
25	-	20	=	5	25
30	-	20	=	10	100
35	-	20	=	15	225
					Total = 700

Standard Deviation = square root of 700/7 = square root of 100 = <u>10</u>

Now, here is a new set of scores. What is the standard deviation of this set?

2   3   10   20   35   35   35

Activity 10.5:
Calculating a Correlation Coefficient

Is there a relationship between the number of pencils and the number of pens a student owns? Use the hypothetical data in Table 10.3 to find out by calculating the Pearson r correlation coefficient:

Table 10.3
PENCILS vs. PENS

Student's Name	Number of Pencils (X)	Number of Pens (Y)	X^2	Y^2	XY
A	3	2	9	4	6
B	6	6	36	36	36
C	5	7	25	49	35
D	2	5	4	25	10
E	6	7	36	49	42
F	2	3	4	9	6
TOTALS	Σ = 24	Σ = 30	Σ = 114	Σ =172	Σ =135

1. Multiply ΣXY by n: = _____

2. Multiply ΣX by ΣY = _____

3. Subtract step 2 from step 1: _____

4. Multiply ΣX^2 by n: _____

5. Square ΣX: _____

6. Subtract step 5 from step 4: _____

7. Multiply ΣY^2 by n: _____

8. Square ΣY: _____

9. Subtract step 8 from step 7: _____

10. Multiply step 6 by step 9: _____

11. Take the square root of step 10 _____

12. Divide step 3 by step 11 _____ (You should get **.75**)

Now, what does this correlation (r) of **.75** tell you? Explain briefly

_____

_____

_____

Activity 10.6
Analyzing Crossbreak Tables

1. Suppose that a researcher wished to study the possible relationship between type of therapeutic approach used by counselors and the institution where the counselor received his or her training. The researcher obtains the data shown in Table 10.4. What conclusions can you draw from the table?

Table 10.4
COMPARISON OF THERAPEUTIC METHOD AND TRAINING INSTITUTION

Training Institution	Method			
	Rogerian	Gestalt	Behavior Modification	Freudian
Happy Valley State	7	20	10	8
Multiversity II	8	6	25	11
College of the Specific	15	10	5	5

_____

_____

2. Table 10.5 indicates how participants in a research project in an inner-city elementary school rated paraprofessionals working in the project. Table 10.7 indicates how they rated each others' cooperation. What do these tables reveal?

Table 10.5
RATINGS OF PARAPROFESSIONALS

	Rating				
	Excellent	Good	Fair	Poor	Total
Teachers	17	7	5	0	29
Paraprofessionals	12	15	1	0	28
Other staff	6	6	2	0	14
Total	35	28	8	0	71

_____

_____

Table 10.6
RATINGS OF PARTICIPANT COOPERATION

	Rating				
	Excellent	**Good**	**Fair**	**Poor**	**Total**
Teachers	5	7	12	6	30
Paraprofessionals	6	12	7	3	28
Other staff	2	3	4	5	14
Total	12	22	23	14	72

Activity 10.7:

Comparing z-Scores

1. Suppose that James received a raw score of **75** on a test where the average (mean) was **73** and the standard deviation was **1,** while Felicia received a score of **82** on a similar test where the mean was **80** and the standard deviation was **2**. Who did better on their test in z-score terms?

2. Assume that a normal distribution of scores has a mean of 50 and a standard deviation of 5. What would be the z-score equivalent for the following raw scores?

    a. **45**   z = _____

    b. **50**   z = _____

    c. **52.5**   z = _____

3. Assume that another normal distribution of scores has a mean of 85 and a standard deviation of 2.5. What would be the raw score equivalent for the following z-scores?

    a. **z = -2**   raw score = _____

    b. **z = +2.33**   raw score = _____

    c. **z = -.33**   raw score = _____

Activity 10.8:
Preparing a 5-number Summary

Listed are percentages of teachers who are fully credentialed. In this activity you will construct a 5-number summary for the percentage of teachers who are fully credentialed for each county in the state of California as published in the San Luis Obispo Tribune (7-29-2001) and shown in the table below.

STATE	RATE	STATE	RATE
Alameda	85.1	Orange	91.3
Alpine	100.0	Placer	97.8
Amador	97.3	Plumas	95.0
Butte	98.2	Riverside	84.5
Calaveras	97.3	Sacramento	95.3
Colusa	92.8	San Benito	83.5
Contra Costa	87.7	San Bernardino	83.1
Del Norte	98.8	San Diego	96.6
El Dorado	96.7	San Francisco	94.4
Fresno	91.2	San Joaquin	86.3
Glenn	95.0	San Luis Obispo	98.1
Humboldt	98.6	San Mateo	88.8
Imperial	79.8	Santa Barbara	95.5
Inyo	94.4	Santa Clara	84.6
Kern	85.1	Santa Cruz	89.6
Kings	85.0	Shasta	97.5
Lake	95.0	Sierra	88.5
Lassen	89.6	Siskiyou	97.7
Los Angeles	74.7	Solano	87.3
Madera	91.0	Sonoma	96.5
Marin	96.8	Stanislaus	94.4
Mariposa	95.5	Sutter	89.3
Mendicino	97.2	Tehama	97.3
Merced	87.8	Trinity	97.5
Modoc	94.6	Tulare	87.6
Mono	95.9	Tuolomne	98.5
Monterey	84.6	Ventura	92.1
Napa	90.8	Yolo	94.6
Nevada	93.9	Yuba	91.6

Construct a 5-number summary for this data set, and draw the corresponding boxplot. Comment on features of the display.

Activity 10.9:
Summarizing Salaries

Shown below are salaries for administrators and teachers in a hypothetical secondary school district. Discussions over a possible salary increase are at an impasse. If you were the chair of the teacher's negotiating team for salary increases for the coming year, which measure of central tendency (mean, median, or mode) would you want to present to the arbitrator? Explain.

John Thomas, Principal	$86,500.00
Alice Waters, Asst. Principal	$64,000.00
Doris Adams, Head Counselor	$52,500.00
Alice Johns, Asst. Principal	$72,000.00
Joan Jeter, Teacher	$32,500.00
Barbara Ho, Teacher	$47,000.00
Susan Sing, Teacher	$49,325.00
Bobbie Davis, Teacher	$37,000.00
Jean Ellis, teacher	$36,500.00
Bill Hong, Teacher	$41,000.00
Susan Sadler, Teacher	$36,325.00
Allison Davis, Teacher	$34,000.00
Bruce Owyoung, Teacher	$34,000.00
Sallie Sucre, Teacher	$34,000.00
Theodore Adams, Teacher	$34,000.00
Danny Wong, Teacher	$34,000.00
Jesus Contreras, Teacher	$34,000.00
David Ellis, teacher	$34,000.00
Dan Simpson, Teacher	$34,000.00
Philip Contrepper, Teacher	$34,000.00

Activity 10.10:
Comparing Scores

In this activity, you will compare the final examination scores of students in different subjects and how they compare to other student sin those classes.

	BIOLOGY MEAN = 78; STANDARD DEVIATION=2	HISTORY MEAN = 82; STANDARD DEVIATION=5	STATISTICS MEAN = 74; STANDARD DEVIATION=3
A	72	80	80
B	78	84	78
C	75	92	77
D	80	77	71
E	80	75	76
F	71	70	75
G	77	88	79
H	79	87	75
I	81	90	77.5
J	84	79	74

For each of the following, convert the student's final exam scores to standard scores.

1. Which student did best overall? Can this be decided? If so, how?
2. How did the best student in biology do compared to the best student in History? In Statistics?
3. Student "G" received a score of 77 in Biology, Student "C" also received a score of 77 in Statistics. Are the scores equivalent? Should they each receive the same letter grade (A, B, C, etc.)? Explain your reasoning.
4. What percentage of students did better than Student "H" in Biology? Than Student "A" in History? Than Student "J" in Statistics?
5. What is noteworthy, if anything, about Student "C?"

Activity 10.11:
Custodial Times

Data on the length of time it takes custodians at a large urban school district to complete various tasks suggests a normal distribution with the following means and standard deviations (SD)

   a. mop a floor: mean = 12 minutes; SD = 2 minutes
   b. clean a lavatory: mean = 19 minutes; SD = 3 minutes
   c. clean a classroom: mean = 8 minutes; SD = 1 minute
   d. empty trash containers: mean = 20 minutes; SD = 5 minutes
   e. wash windows in administrative offices: mean = 15 minutes; SD = 5 minutes

   Due to budgetary cutbacks, the administration ahs decided to release those custodians who fall in the following percentages with regard to completing at least three of the above-listed tasks:

   a. the bottom 5 percent
   b. the bottom 10 percent
   c. the bottom 3 percent
   d. the bottom 15 percent
   e. the bottom 4 percent

   There are six custodians employed by the district. Here are their times for completing each of the above-mentioned tasks. Based on this information, which custodians (if any) should be released?

CUSTODIAN	A. MOP FLOOR	B. CLEAN LAVATORY	C. CLEAN CLASSROOM	D. EMPTY TRASH	E. WASH WINDOWS
Alice	11.8 minutes	19 minutes	7 minutes	30 minutes	22 minutes
Samuel	11 minutes	17.8 minutes	9.2 minutes	33 minutes	17 minutes
Rosa	13 minutes	22 minutes	10 minutes	34.5 minutes	18.4 minutes
Tom	13.9 minutes	23.8 minutes	9.8 minutes	37 minutes	19 minutes
Gus	15.8 minutes	25 minutes	10.1 minutes	37.9 minutes	15 minutes
Adam	14 minutes	25.4 minutes	12 minutes	20 minutes	15.8 minutes

Activity 10.12:
Collecting Data

In this activity, you will work in groups of 4-5 students to collect data that will provide information about how many hours per week, on average, your classmates spend time on various activities.

1. Use the plan developed in Activity 6.5 to collect data on each of the following:

   a. Preparing for class
   b. Participating in athletics
   c. Participating in social activities
   d. Sleeping
   e. Other

2. Summarize the resulting data using appropriate numerical and graphical summaries. Be sure to address both center and variability.

3. Compare your data with that of two other groups, and prepare a comparison chart to present visually to the class for discussion and comparison.

CHAPTER 11: Inferential Statistics

Activity 11.1:
Probability

1. Take a coin and test the hypothesis that the coin is dishonest, that is, that it comes up heads more times than it comes up tails.

2. Flip the coin four times. Record the number of heads here: _____

3. Based on just this amount of data, would you accept or reject the hypothesis?
   Accept _____ Reject _____ Why?_____

4. Suppose that you had gotten four heads (maybe you did). Would you then accept or reject the hypothesis? _____ Why? _____

5. Now flip the same coin four more times and record the number of heads. Do this 16 times. (Note: Each set of four flips can be considered a sample. For each sample, the possible number of heads is 0, 1, 2, 3, or 4.)

Flip Number	Number of Heads	Flip Number	Number of Heads
1		9	
2		10	
3		11	
4		12	
5		13	
6		14	
7		15	
8		16	

6. Next, tally the number of times each possible outcome occurred. Then change each to a percent by dividing by 16.

Outcome	Number of times outcome occurred	Percent
0 heads		
1 head		
2 heads		
3 heads		
4 heads		

7. If you were to use several coins and many more samples, you would (almost certainly) arrive at a table that presents the results to be expected with an honest coin. It would be very similar to that shown below.

Outcome	Percent	Probability
0 heads	6	.06
1 head	25	.25
2 heads	38	.38
3 heads	25	.25
4 heads	6	.06
Total	100	1.00

8. These percentages are actually probabilities. They tell us how often we would expect each outcome to occur with an honest coin. Now, return to your original sample (the first set of four flips of your coin). Would you now change your interpretation in any way?

Yes _____ No _____. If yes, how so? _____

If not, why not? _____

_____

_____

Activity 11.2:
Learning to Read a *t*-Table

There are certain probabilities that researchers take as indicative of a stable nonchance relationship. If the probability of obtaining a particular result or relationship in a sample is less than **.05** (one chance in **20**), we customarily consider it to be *statistically significant* -- that is, as probably not due to chance. If the probability is less than 5 percent (for example, 1 percent), we can be even more confident that we are not simply dealing with chance. These values (1 percent and 5 percent) are frequently referred to as *levels of statistical significance.*

Hence, when a research report states that a particular result (e.g., a difference in means) or relationship (e.g., a correlation coefficient) is significant at the 5 percent level, it means that the chances of the finding being simply a fluke (due to the particular sample that was used) are less than 5 in 100. It means that the relationship or result is worth noting and tentatively acceptable as a reproducible relationship for a specified population. Note that *statistical significance* is not the same things a *practical significance,* however.

A t-test is used to test the statistical significance of a difference between two means. A *t*-table shows the value of *t* required for a particular result to be considered statistically significant at various degrees of freedom (d.f.). Once the appropriate d.f. have been determined and the *t* value has been calculated, the table indicates what a calculated *t* value must be (the critical *t* value) to be considered statistically significant at different levels of significance (e.g., **.05, .01**).

For example, a *t* value calculated for a sample having **10 d.f.** using a one-tailed (i.e., directional) test must be at least **1.812** to be considered statistically significant at the **.05** level, as shown in the normal curve and table presented below. What must the *t* value be for such a sample to be statistically at the **.01** level? _____ Now, suppose another sample has **25** degrees of freedom. What must be the t value be to be considered statistically significant at the **.05** level? _____ At the **.01** level? _____

Degrees of Freedom	Proportion in Critical Region			
	.005	.10	.05	.01
1	63.657	3.078	6.314	31.821
5	4.032	1.476	2.015	3.365
10	3.169	1.372	1.812	2.764
25	2.787	1.316	1.708	2.485
40	2.704	1.303	1.684	2.423
60	2.660	1.296	1.671	2.390

Activity 11.3:
Calculate a *t*-Test

A researcher wishes to compare the achievement of two groups of students who are taught social studies by two different methods. Group I (n = **26**) was taught by the inquiry method. Group II (n = **26**) was taught by the lecture method. The average (mean) score of each group on a 100-point final examination was **85** for the lecture group (standard deviation = **3** points) and **87** for the inquiry group (standard deviation = **2** points).

Use **Table D.2** in the Appendix in the text to calculate a *t*-test for the difference in means. Follow the steps in Table D.2 to fill in the table below (we have filled in the first two lines).

	Inquiry Group	Lecture Group
Mean	87	85
Standard deviation (SD)	2	3
Standard error of the mean (SEM)		
Standard error of the difference (SED)		

$t =$ _____   Degrees of freedom (d.f.) is obtained by $n_1 + n_2 - 2 = 26 +$ 26 − 2 = 50

Consult the table below to determine if the obtained *t*-value is statistically significant at the **.05** level.

	Proportion in Critical Region			
Degrees of Freedom	**.005**	**.10**	**.05**	**.01**
1	63.657	3.078	6.314	31.821
5	4.032	1.476	2.015	3.365
10	3.169	1.372	1.812	2.764
25	2.787	1.316	1.708	2.485
40	2.704	1.303	1.684	2.423
60	2.660	1.296	1.671	2.390

The difference between the inquiry and the lecture groups was _____ or was not _____ statistically significant

*Note: This exercise is designed to illustrate the procedure. When the number of cases in each group, as here, is less than 30, a somewhat different formula should be used. It can be found in any basic statistics text.

Activity 11.4:
Perform a Chi-Square Test

Chi-square is the most commonly used statistic for determining whether a relationship between two categorical variables is statistically significant. The formula for calculating chi-square is:

$$X^2 = \sum \frac{(f_O - f_E)^2}{f_E}$$

Suppose a researcher wishes to determine whether, at selected high schools, there is a relationship between number of students enrolling in physical education courses and participation in intramural sports. The data might look like that shown in Table 11.4.

Table 11.4

University	Number of students enrolling in physical education courses	Number of students participating in intramural sports	Totals
Alpha	70 (60)	30 (40)	100
Beta	130	70	
Kappa	160	140	
Totals	360		

The numbers in each of the cells in the table represent the observed frequencies (f_O). To obtain chi-square, go through the following steps:

1. Add up (total) both columns and rows. For example, the total number of students enrolling in physical education courses is **360**. Enter the totals in the table.

2. Calculate the proportion of the total frequency that falls in <u>each</u> row and column. Thus, you should see that Alpha University has **100/600**, or **1/6** of the total number of students.

3. Multiply each row proportion by its column total. These are expected frequencies (f_E). Thus, for Alpha University, the expected frequencies for the number of students enrolling in physical education courses is **1/6(360) = 60**. For the number of students participating in intramural sports, it is **1/6(240) = 40**. Enter these in parentheses, as I did for Alpha University, in each of the other cells.

4. For each cell, subtract the expected frequency (f_E) from the obtained frequency (f_O), square the result, and then divide it by (f_E). Fill in the results below.

    $(70 - 60)^2/60 = 10^2/60 = 100/60 = 1.67$

    $(30 - 40)^2/40 = -10^2/40 = 100/40 = $ _____

    $(130 - 120)^2/120 = 10^2/120 = 100/120 = $ _____

$(70 - 80)^2/80 = -10^2/80 = 100/80 =$ _____

$(160 - 180)^2/180 = -20^2/180 = 400/180 =$ _____

$(140 - 120)^2/120 = 20^2/120 = 400/120 =$ _____

5. Next, total these six values, as symbolized by

$$X^2 = \sum \frac{(fO - fE)^2}{fE}$$

to obtain a chi-square value of _____ (You should get **11.80**)

6. Now, to determine whether this value is statistically significant, compare the calculated value of chi-square to the values in the chi-square table below. To determine the degrees of freedom (d.f.), multiply the number of rows minus one (r – 1) times the number of columns minus one (c – 1). In this case, it would be **(3 – 1) x (2 – 1) = 2.** The chi-square table indicates that, with two d.f., a value of _____ is required for a result to be statistically significant. Is the value you obtained (**11.80**) statistically significant? Yes _____ No _____

			α LEVELS		
DEGREES OF FREEDOM	.10	.05	.02	.01	.001
1	2.71	3.84	5.41	6.64	10.83
2	4.60	5.99	7.82	9.21	13.82
3	6.25	7.82	9.84	11.34	16.27
4	7.78	9.49	11.67	13.28	18.46
5	9.24	11.07	13.39	15.09	20.52
10	15.99	18.31	21.16	23.21	29.59
20	28.41	31.41	35.02	37.57	45.32
25	34.38	37.65	41.57	44.31	52.62
30	40.26	43.77	47.96	50.89	59.70

To be significant, the x^2 obtained from the data must be equal to or larger than the value shown in the table.

Activity 11.5:
Conduct a *t*-Test

Identify a group of at least 10 people (classmates, friends, neighbors, etc.).

1. Divide the group into two roughly equal sub-groups, based on some characteristic such as gender, age, height, etc.

2. Ask each person independently to pick a number from 1 to 9.

3. Calculate the mean of these numbers for each group.

4. Write the difference between the means of the two groups here. _____

5. Calculate a *t*-test for the difference in means using Table D-2 in the appendix of the text. Use the portion of the *t*-table shown below to determine the statistical significance of the difference in means that you obtained for the two groups.

Degrees of Freedom	Proportion in Critical Region			
	.005	.10	.05	.01
1	63.657	3.078	6.314	31.821
5	4.032	1.476	2.015	3.365
10	3.169	1.372	1.812	2.764
25	2.787	1.316	1.708	2.485
40	2.704	1.303	1.684	2.423
60	2.660	1.296	1.671	2.390

Were the results statistically significant? Yes _____ No _____

6. What basic assumption must be met to justify using a t-test?_____

_____

_____

7. Was it met? Yes _____ No _____ Explain why it was or was not. _____

_____

_____

_____

Activity 11.6:
The Big Game

Ms. Jones has recently failed Bobby Thomasinki, Central High School's star pitcher, on his last exam in U.S. History, making him ineligible to play in the school's championship baseball game that will occur in two weeks. Bobby's parents have asked for a conference with you to discuss the matter. Bobby received a score of 16 out of 20 points on the exam (which consisted of 20 true-false questions). Ms. Jones believes that Bobby must have cheated, as he had failed the three previous exams she had given in the course, and had never received more than 8 points on any of these other true-false exams. Bobby claims that he was lucky, that he passed the exam by guessing. Ms. Jones says this simply could not happen, and presents the information in the table below as evidence to support her belief. A total of 500 of Ms. Jones students have taken this exam over the last five years. Bobby's parents say it could happen, and that he therefore should be allowed to play in the championship game. You think that, given the facts of the case, it was indeed unlikely that Bobby could have passed the exam by guessing. Use probability to support your decision.

PAST PERFORMANCE OF STUDENTS ON THIS QUIZ

NO. OF CORRECT RESPONSES	NUMBER OF STUDENTS	PROPORTION OF STUDENTS	NUMBER OF CORRECT RESPONSES	NUMBER OF STUDENTS	PROPORTION OF STUDENTS
0	0	.000	11	79	.158
1	0	.000	12	61	.122
2	1	.002	13	39	.078
3	1	.002	14	18	.036
4	2	.004	15	7	.014
5	8	.016	16	1	.002
6	18	.036	17	1	.002
7	37	.074	18	0	.000
8	58	.116	19	0	.000
9	81	.162	20	0	.000
10	88	.176			

1. Bobby received a score of 16. Do you think he was just guessing? (Hint: What is the probability of a student getting a score at least as high as Bobby's score, based on the past performance of students who have taken this exam? Do you think these past records reflect more than guessing?)

2. What would you decide in Bobby's case? Was he guessing? What other possibilities might explain his high score? Would you allow him to play in the big game?

CHAPTER 12: Statistics in Perspective

Activity 12.1:
Statistical vs. Practical Significance

In each of the following, discuss whether the result or relationship is likely to be practically significant (PS), and then explain your reasoning.

1. A researcher finds that a particular relationship can occur by chance about 20 times in 100.

2. A researcher finds that students who use a new biology textbook recently purchased by the school district scored an average of 20 percent higher on an end-of-the-course examination.

3. A medical researcher finds that the use of a certain drug decreases the incidence of a life-threatening drug among a group of senior citizens by 3 percent.

4. A small appliance store finds that advertising in the local neighborhood newspaper increases her sales each week by 1 percent.

5. A new method of teaching five-year-olds how to tie their shoes results in their being able to do so three weeks earlier than similar five-year-olds not taught this method.

6. A researcher finds that a correlation of .18 has only a 1 in 1,000 likelihood of occurring by chance.

Activity 12.2:
Appropriate Techniques

Match the technique in Column A with the appropriate description from Column B

Column A	Column B
1. Effect size	a. A graphic way to show all of the information about a group
2. Inferential statistics	b. An unusual score
3. Known groups	c. Takes into account the size of a difference, regardless of whether it is statistically significant
4. Scatterplot	
5. Crossbreak table	d. Graphic technique for illustrating a relationship between quantitative variables within a single group
6. Test of statistical significance	
7. Outlier	e. A means of assessing generalizability
8. Confidence interval	
	f. Often a useful frame of reference to use in interpreting the magnitude of a difference between means of two groups
	g. Should be reported in addition to (or instead of) significance levels whenever possible
	h. Sometimes may be insignificant in any real or educational sense
	i. A graphic used to illustrate relationships among categorical data

Activity 12.3:
Interpret the Data

Review Activity 11.5 and then respond to the following.

1. What does the difference in means tell you? _____

_____

2. What does the *t*-test tell you? _____

3. What other indexes might be useful? _____

4. What would they tell you? _____

_____

Activity 12.4:
Collect Some Data

Imagine that you and a colleague conducted a study with two large random samples of Swedes and Germans. You find a mean I.Q. difference of six points in favor of the Swedes. Assume that this difference was statistically significant at the .05 level.

1. Give these hypothetical "results" to five friends or acquaintances and ask them what they think this all means. Summarize the responses of each below.

Person #1 _____

_____

Person #2 _____

_____

Person #3 _____

_____

Person #4 _____

_____

Person #5 _____

_____

2. Summarize similarities and differences between the responses and record what you learned below.

_____

_____

_____

_____

(Be sure to tell your participants afterward that these results are fake.)

96

CHAPTER 13: Experimental Research

Activity 13.1:
Group Experimental Research Questions

Which of the following questions would lend themselves well to group experimental research?

1. What factors influence job success?

2. Which is more effective in reducing the anxiety of clients, client-centered or traditional therapy?

3. Does personal counseling improve student achievement?

4. Why do teachers experience burnout?

5. What is the relationship (if any) between teacher gender and student achievement?

6. How did science textbooks used in the 1940s compare with those used today?

7. Do students like history more if taught by the case study or the inquiry method?

8. What makes a good high school counselor?

9. What sorts of problems do most first-year teachers face?

Activity 13.2:
Designing an Experiment

Fizz Laboratories, a pharmaceutical company, has developed a new pain-relief medication. Sixty patients suffering from arthritis and needing pain relief are available. Each patient will be treated and then asked an hour later, "About what percentage of pain relief did you experience?" Work with another student to prepare answers to each of the following questions or tasks.

1. Why should Fizz not simply administer the new drug and record the patient's responses?

2. Draw the design below of an experiment to compare the drug's effectiveness with that of aspirin and a placebo.

3. Should patients be told which group they are in? How would knowledge probably affect their reactions?

4. If patients are not told which treatment they are receiving, the experiment is single-blind. Should this experiment also be double-blind? Explain.

Activity 13.3:
Characteristics of Experimental Research

Match the concept from Column A with the correct definition from Column B.

Column A	Column B
1. Experimental group	a. Refers to the result(s) or outcome(s) being studied
2. Control group	b. A process wherein every member of a population has an equal chance to be a member of the sample
3. Random selection	
4. Random assignment	c. An unplanned-for variable that may be the cause of a result observed in a study
5. Independent variable	d. The group that does not receive a treatment in an experiment
6. Dependent variable	
7. Extraneous variable	e. A process of pairing two individuals whose scores on a particular measure are similar
8. Matching	f. Sometimes referred to as the treatment variable in a study
	g. Every individual who is participating in an experiment has an equal chance of being assigned to any of the experimental or control conditions being compared
	h. The sample of individuals participating in an experiment
	i. The group that received a treatment of some sort in an experiment

Activity 13.4:
Random Selection vs. Random Assignment

Described below are four examples of randomization. Write **RS** if random selection is involved; **RA** if random assignment is involved; **B** if both random selection and random assignment are involved; or **O** if no randomization is involved.

1. _____ Using all fifth-grade classes in the campus demonstration school, a researcher divides the students in each class into two groups by drawing their names from a hat.

2. _____ All students with learning handicaps in a school district are identified and the names of 50 are pulled from a hat. The first 25 are given an experimental treatment, and the remainder are taught as usual.

3. _____ All third-grade students in an elementary school district who are being taught to read by the literature method are identified, as are all students who are being taught with basal readers. The names of all students in each group are placed in a hat and then 50 students from each group are selected.

4. _____ Students in three classes with computer assistance are compared with three classes not using computers.

CHAPTER 14: Single-Subject Research

Activity 14.1:
Single-Subject Research Questions

Which of the following questions would lend themselves well to single-subject research?

1. How do students view the president of the university?

2. Which is more effective in helping students to learn a language, individual instruction or language laboratories?

3. What is the daily routine of a high school guidance counselor?

4. How are women portrayed in advertisements in popular magazines?

5. How can Jimmy Thomas be encouraged to speak up more in class?

6. Why do some students have trouble learning to read?

7. What makes a good teacher lose his or her enthusiasm for teaching?

8. Is praise an effective technique to use with disruptive students?

Activity 14.2:
Characteristics of Single-Subject Research

Match the concept from Column A with the correct definition from Column B.

Column A	Column B
1. Baseline	1. Single-subject designs are weak when it comes to this
2. Data point	2. Starting point for a single-subject study
3. Condition line	3. Indicate(s) where the intervention conditions change in a single-subject study
4. Comparison of two or more groups	4. Represents the data collected at various times during a single-subject study
5. Treatment condition	5. The end point of a single-subject study
6. Generalizability	6. Important if single-subject studies are to have external validity
7. Replication	7. The intervention in a single-subject study
8. Single-subject research	8. Do(es) not occur in single-subject research
	9. Used to study changes in behavior of an individual after exposure to a treatment of some sort

Activity 14.3:
Analyze Some Single Subject Data

Alicia Morales, a sixth-grade teacher in Sarasota, Florida, wishes that Jamie Brown, one of her students, would pay more attention in class (behavior 1). She also would like to see him volunteer to answer questions more frequently (behavior 2), as well as speak directly to other students during class discussions (behavior 3). Consequently, she decides to use a multiple-baseline design to see if she can increase these behaviors by systematically praising Jamie (the "treatment" she plans to use) whenever one of these behaviors occurs. She is fortunate in that she has a teacher's aide who can observe Jamie while class is in session and she is teaching. After three weeks, the results of the intervention are shown below: What do you think? Was the treatment effective?

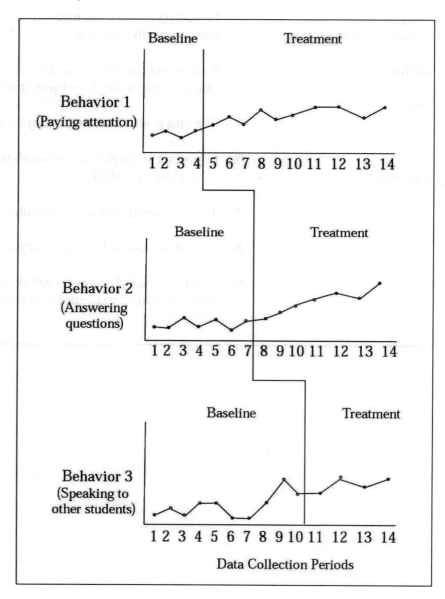

CHAPTER 15: Correlational Research

Activity 15.1: Correlational Research Questions

Activity 15.2: What Kind of Correlation?

Activity 15.3: Think Up an Example

Activity 15.4: Match the Correlation Coefficient to its Scatterplot

Activity 15.5: Calculate a Correlation Coefficient

Activity 15.6: Construct a Scatterplot

Activity 15.7: Correlation in Everyday Life

Activity 15.8: Regression

Activity 15.1:
Correlational Research Questions

Which of the following questions would lend themselves well to correlational research?

1. What are student attitudes toward environmental organizations?

2. Do students like history more if taught by the inquiry method?

3. What does a high school football coach do when he isn't coaching?

4. What sorts of themes appear in the editorials in the *New York Times*?

5. Does early success in school lead to financial success in adulthood?

6. Is teacher praise related to student achievement?

Activity 15.2:
What Kind of Correlation?

Would each of the following be positively, negatively, or not correlated?

1. _____ height and weight of people ages 1-18

2. _____ weight and speed of people ages 20-50

3. _____ health and length of life

4. _____ running speed and taste for mystery novels

5. _____ size and strength of people ages 10-30

6. _____ achievement in school and absenteeism

7. _____ television viewing (in hours) and reading achievement

8. _____ food intake at a meal and stomach comfort

9. _____ height and life expectancy

Activity 15.3:
Think Up an Example

In the space provided, write an example of two things that would have:

black clouds / rain strom.

1. A strong positive correlation: watering gurden and veggies

2. A strong negative correlation: body odor and getting a hot date

3. A weak positive correlation: Student success and upstairs/downstairs class room ⊖ (trafluor)

#teeth + level education

4. A weak negative correlation: balloons and better party ⊕

5. Little or no correlation: red house and more cats

Activity 15.4:
Match the Correlation Coefficient to its Scatterplot

Shown below are eight scatterplots. In the space alongside each, write in the appropriate correlation coefficient from the following list:

r = .90; *r* = .65; *r* = .35; *r* = .00; *r* = -.90; *r* = -.75; *r* = -.50; *r* = -.10

a)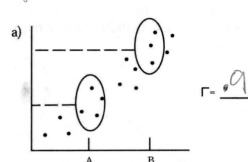

r = .9

e)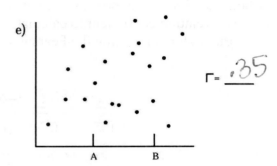

r = .35

b)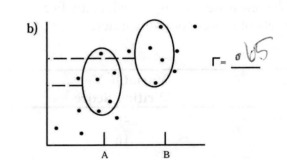

r = .65

f)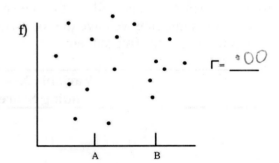

r = .00

c)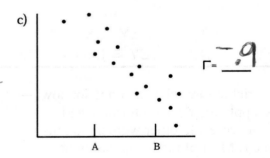

r = -.9

g)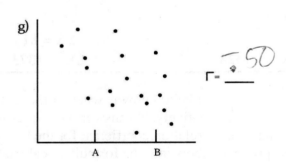

r = -.50

d)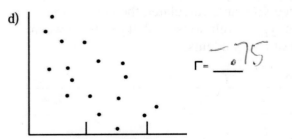

r = -.75

h)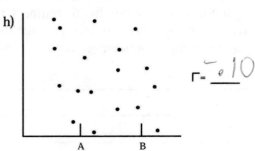

r = -.10

Activity 15.5:
Calculate a Correlation Coefficient

Actually, there are many different correlation coefficients, each applying to a particular circumstance and each calculated by means of a different computational formula. The one we will use in this exercise is the one most frequently used: the Pearson product-moment coefficient of correlation. It is symbolized by the lowercase letter r. When the data for both variables are expressed in terms of quantitative scores, the Pearson r is the appropriate correlation coefficient to calculate. It is designed for use with interval or ratio data. The formula for calculating the Pearson r coefficient is:

$$r = \frac{n\Sigma XY - (\Sigma X)(\Sigma Y)}{\sqrt{[n\Sigma X^2 - (\Sigma X)^2][n\Sigma Y^2 - (\Sigma Y)^2]}}$$

The Pearson formula looks a lot more complicated than it really is. It does have a lot of steps to follow before you actually get to the end, but each step is easy to calculate. For this exercise, let's imagine we have the following sets of scores for two variables -- reading and writing -- for five students:

Student Name	Variable X— Reading Score	Variable Y— Writing Score
Al	20	20
Beth	18	16
Cathy	18	20
Dave	15	12
Ed	10	10
Total	$\Sigma X = 81$	$\Sigma Y = 78$
$\Sigma XY = 1328$	$\Sigma X^2 = 1373$	$\Sigma Y^2 = 1300$

What we would like to know is whether these two variables are related, and if so, how — positively or negatively. To answer these questions, apply the Pearson formula and calculate the correlation coefficient for the two sets of scores. In other words, plug the appropriate numbers into the formula to calculate the r. Most of the computation has already been done for you and is provided in the bottom two rows of boxes. (See Appendix D at the end of the textbook for a step-by-step example of how to calculate a correlation coefficient using this formula.) Once you have calculated the correlation coefficient, describe below in one sentence the type of relationship that exists between reading and writing scores among this sample of five students:

_____

_____

_____

Activity 15.6:
Construct a Scatterplot

In this activity, you are to construct a scatterplot and calculate a correlation coefficient to determine if there is a relationship between the number of hours a student works and his or her grade point average (GPA).

    a. Is there a relationship between hours worked and GPA?

    b. If so, is it positive or negative? Is it strong or weak? Explain in words what the scatterplot reveals.

    c. Calculate the correlation coefficient (Follow the steps shown in Appendix A)

    d. Are there any outliers? What do they suggest?

STUDENT	HOURS WORKED	GRADE POINT AVERAGE
ALPHONSO	30	1.42
ROBERTO	21	2.75
ELOISE	12	3.64
FELIX	18	2.40
JACK	9	3.75
OSCAR	0	4.00
WILLIE	20	3.10
DAVID	24	3.25
SUSAN	14	2.87
FELICIA	19	2.20
BETTYE	28	1.75
JUAN	3	3.88
ANGELINA	9	1.52
JESUS	16	2.81
ELLIE	18	2.66
SAM	30	0.87
CHIN	21	2.99
TOGUIAS	22	2.58
JEREMIAH	23	2.85
JOSHUA	9	4.00

Activity 15.7:
Correlation in Everyday Life

Below we present a number of everyday sayings that suggest relationships. What correlations do they suggest? Are they positive or negative?

1. A fool and his money are soon parted.

2. As the twig is bent, so grows the tree.

3. You can't grow grass on a busy street.

4. Virtue is its own reward.

5. What fails to destroy me makes me stronger.

6. To get along, go along.

7. You can't make an omelet without breaking some eggs.

8. You can't make a silk purse out of a sow's ear.

9. All that glitters is not gold.

10. If at first you don't succeed, try, try again.

Activity 15.8:
Regression

In this activity, you are to use the table below to complete the tasks listed below the table.

Percentages of public school students in 4th grade in 1996 and in 8th grade in 2002 who were at or above the proficient level in mathematics for eight western states are shown in the table below:

STATE	4TH GRADE (1996)	8TH GRADE (2002)
ARIZONA	15	21
CALIFORNIA	11	18
HAWAII	16	16
MONTANA	22	37
NEW MEXICO	13	13
OREGON	21	32
UTAH	23	26
WYOMING	19	25

a. Construct a scatterplot and discuss the interesting features of the plot.

b. Find the equation of the least-squares line that summarizes the relationship between x = 1966 4th grade math proficiency and y = 2000 8th grade math proficiency math percentage.

c. Nevada, a western state not included in the data, had a 1996 4th grade math proficiency of 14%. What would you predict for Nevada's 2000 8th grade math proficiency percentage? How does your prediction compare to the actual 8th grade math value of 20 for Nevada?

CHAPTER 16: Causal-Comparative Research

Activity 16.1:
Causal-Comparative Research Questions

Which of the following questions would lend themselves well to causal-comparative research?

1. How many students were enrolled in Psych 101 this semester?

2. Which subjects do high school students like least?

3. How do elementary school teachers teach phonics?

4. Are two-year-old girls more aggressive than two-year-old boys?

5. Do "C" students do better in athletics than "A" and "B" students?

6. How might Jimmy Thomas be helped to read?

7. Is teacher enthusiasm related to student success in academic classes?

8. What is the best way to teach arithmetic?

Activity 16.2:
Experiment or Causal-Comparative Study

In this activity, you will work with a partner to identify different types of statistical studies.

1. For each of the following studies, decide whether it is an experiment, a casual-comparative study, or neither.

    a. A Stanford University study of starting salaries for college graduates found that computer science majors had the highest salaries ($42,500), while communications majors had the lowest ($25,600).

    b. A European study of 1,500 men and women with exceptionally high levels of the amino acid homocysteine found that these individuals had double the risk of heart disease. However, the risk was substantially lower for those in the study who were given vitamin B supplements.

    c. Researchers at Columbia University found that the genetic modification of corn known as Bt corn increases the secretion of insecticide through plant roots into the soil.

    d. A New Zealand study found no relationship between years of education and income.

    e. A researcher found that playing soccer did not help swimmers increase their time in competitive races.

    f. A breast cancer study questioned 20,000 women about how they spend their leisure time. The health of these women was tracked over the next ten years. Those women who said they exercised regularly were found to have a lower incidence of breast cancer.

2. If it is an experiment or casual-comparative study, describe the group or groups studied.

Activity 16.3:
Causal-Comparative Versus Experimental Hypotheses

Listed below are a number of hypotheses. Which could be studied best as an *experiment* and which could be carried out best as a *casual-comparative* study?

1. *Hypothesis #1*: Deaf high school students in residential settings who receive instruction in English through a combination of signed English and American Sign Language (ASL) will demonstrate higher levels of written English than those taught using only signed English.

   Experimental study_____ Casual-comparative study_____

2. *Hypothesis #2*: Adult homosexual males have had greater exposure to sexual abuse in childhood than adult heterosexual males.

   Experimental study_____ Casual-comparative study_____

3. *Hypothesis #3*: Male high school students who participate in a four-week simulation of pregnancy will subsequently demonstrate more responsible attitudes toward parenthood than similar students not participating in the simulation.

   Experimental study_____ Casual-comparative study_____

Activity 16.4:
Analyze Some Causal-Comparative Data

Just prior to the commencement of the fall semester at a large Midwestern university, Professor Judith Brown, an ardent feminist who has a Ph.D in statistics, gets into a discussion with one of her male colleagues about who are better statistics students, males or females. She hypothesizes that the females in her classes, on average, will outperform the males.

Listed in Table 16.1 are the scores on the final examination earned by each of the 24 students (12 females and 12 males) in her introductory class. Calculate the mean (the average) score for both the male and the female students in Dr. Brown's class. Is there a difference? If there is a difference, can Dr. Brown argue that gender is the cause of this apparent difference in ability (indeed, that her hypothesis is correct)? Explain your conclusion in the space provided under the table.

Table 16.1:
Scores on a Final Examination

Females	Males
70	90
75	68
93	91
84	80
65	77
87	80
90	91
95	76
88	75
78	62
86	77
84	87
Total =	Total =
Female mean =	Male mean =

_____

_____

_____

_____

_____

CHAPTER 17: Survey Research

Activity 17.1:
Survey Research Questions

Which of the following questions would lend themselves well to survey research?

1. How do sophomore students feel about the new counseling program?

2. In what ways were delinquent and non-delinquent boys similar and different during the 1930s?

3. Is inquiry teaching more effective than lectures in the teaching of sociology?

4. How much college tuition are parents able and willing to pay?

yes? 5. How many single mothers were on welfare in Contra Costa County during the past nine months?

6. Do professors think it is ethical to require graduate students to participate in a professor's research project?

yes? 7. What does a high school principal do each day?

Questionaire Survey

Activity 17.2:
Types of Surveys

Match the concept from Column A with the correct statement from Column B

Column A	Column B
1. Longitudinal survey _d_	a. The researcher surveys the same sample of individuals at different times during the course of a study
2. Cross-sectional survey _i_	
3. Trend study _g_	b. An advantage of this type of survey is that it gives the researcher access to a sample that might be otherwise hard to reach
4. Cohort study _f_	
5. Panel study _a_	c. Used whenever a researcher has access to all (or most) of the members of a particular group in one place
6. Census _j, c_	
7. Mail survey _b_	d. Researcher collects information at different points in time in order to study changes over time
8. Personal interview _e, c_	
	e. Probably the most effective way to enlist the cooperation of the respondents in a survey
	f. Researcher obtains different samples of a particular population whose members do not change over the course of the study
	g. Researcher samples a population whose members may change over time
	h. Major purpose is to describe the characteristics of an invited sample
	i. Researcher collects information from a sample that has been drawn from a predetermined population
	j. An entire population is surveyed

Activity 17.3:
Open- vs. Closed-Ended Questions

In the space below each of the following open-ended question, see if you can change them to closed-ended questions.

1. What was your favorite subject when you were in elementary school?

2. What makes a good teacher?

3. What factors contributed to the election of George W. Bush in 2000?

4. Why is it that many poor people in the United States today cannot improve their status?

Activity 17.4:
Conduct a Survey

How do the grades that students expect to get correspond to the quality of their work in class? In this exercise, you are asked to conduct a survey to find out how other students feel about this question. Contact a sample of at least 25 students in two different courses (a total of 50) and ask them to rate the quality of their work in one of their courses and tell you the grade they expect to get in that course. Use an expanded copy of the form below.

RATING SCALE

A = Distinguished
B = Superior
C = Average
D = Below Average
F = Failure

COURSE #1

FIRST NAME OF STUDENT	RATING OF WORK IN CLASS	EXPECTED GRADE

COURSE #2

FIRST NAME OF STUDENT	RATING OF WORK IN CLASS	EXPECTED GRADE

Use the table below to record the number and percent of the total for each grade. How do the ratings compare? What conclusions can you draw?

COURSE #1

FIRST NAME OF STUDENT	RATING OF WORK IN CLASS	EXPECTED GRADE
A		
B		
C		
D		
F		

COURSE #2

FIRST NAME OF STUDENT	RATING OF WORK IN CLASS	EXPECTED GRADE
A		
B		
C		
D		
F		

CHAPTER 18: The Nature of Qualitative Research

Activity 18.1: Qualitative Research Questions

Activity 18.2: Qualitative vs. Quantitative Research

Activity 18.3: Approaches to Qualitative Research

Activity 18.1:
Qualitative Research Questions

Which of the following questions would lend themselves well to qualitative research?

1. Do students learn more in a language laboratory than they do in a teacher-directed classroom?

2. What sorts of conditioning drills do physical education teachers use?

3. How do elementary teachers teach children to read?

4. Is client-centered therapy more effective than traditional therapy with teenagers?

5. What kinds of things do history teachers do as they go about their daily routine?

6. How many district administrators took a sabbatical leave this past year?

7. Is the fingerprinting of student teachers legal?

8. How did teachers teach science during the 1920s?

9. What methods do the volunteer tutors use in the after-school tutoring program?

Activity 18.2:
Qualitative vs. Quantitative Research

In the space provided after each of the characteristics listed below, write "Qualitative" if the characteristic refers primarily to one or more qualitative research methodologies. Write "Quantitative" if the characteristic refers primarily to one or more quantitative research methodologies.

1. A preference for hypotheses that emerge as the study progresses

   _____

2. A preference for precise definitions stated at the outset of the study

   _____

3. A preference for statistical summary of results _____

4. Data is analyzed inductively _____

5. A preference for random techniques for obtaining meaningful samples

   _____

6. A lot of attention devoted to assessing and improving the reliability of scores obtained from instruments _____

7. A willingness to manipulate conditions when studying complex phenomena

   _____

8. The researcher is the key instrument _____

9. Primary reliance is on the researcher to deal with procedural bias

   _____

10. The natural setting is the direct source of data _____

11. Data are collected primarily in the form of numbers _____

Activity 18.3:
Approaches to Qualitative Research

Match the approach to qualitative research listed in Column B with its description in Column A.

Column A: Description	Column B: Approach to Qualitative Research
1. _____ Researchers generally assume that there is some commonality to the perceptions human beings have in how they interpret an experience	a. Biography
2. _____ Description of the cultural behavior of a group or individual	b. Phenomenology
3. _____ Researchers start with an area of study and then allow what is relevant to that area to emerge	c. Grounded theory
	d. Case study
4. _____ Interest is in the experiences of a single individual	e. Ethnography
5. _____ Researcher is interested in studying a particular case only as a means to some larger goal he or she has in mind	
6. _____ Researcher studies an individual's reactions to a particular experience or set of experiences	
7. _____ Researchers doing this type of study use what is known as the *constant comparative* method	
8. _____ Often involves a study of just one classroom or program	

CHAPTER 19: Observation and Interviewing

Activity 19.1:
Observer Roles

Match the role listed in Column B with its description in Column A.

Column A	Column B
1. _____ Researcher observes the activities of a group without in any way becoming a participant in those activities	a. Complete participant
	b. Participant as observer
2. _____ Individual identifies him or herself as a researcher, but does not pretend to be a member of the group being observed	c. Observer as participant
	d. Complete observer
3. _____ This role is sometimes suspect on ethical grounds	
4. _____ Researcher participates fully in the activities of the group being observed	
5. _____ Researcher is least likely to affect the actions of the group in this role	
6. _____ Researcher's identity is not known to any of the individuals he or she is observing	

Activity 19.2:
Types of Interviews

Match the type of interview listed in Column B with its description in Column A. (Note: Some descriptions may apply to more than one type of interview.)

Column A: Description	Column B: Type of Interview
1. _____ Tends to resemble a casual conversation	a. Structured
2. _____Requires the least training of the interviewer	b. Semi-structured
	c. Informal
3. _____ Probably the most difficult of all to conduct	d. Retrospective
4. _____Can be any one of the other three types	
5. _____ Offers the most natural type of situation for the collection of data	
6. _____ Most useful for obtaining information to test the specific hypothesis a researcher wished to investigate	
7. _____ Least likely of the four to provide reliable data for the researcher	

Activity 19.3:
Types of Interview Questions

Match the type of interview question listed in Column B with the appropriate example in Column A.

Column A: Examples	Column B: Type of Interview Question
1. b/c (C) What sorts of things do you do in drama class?	a. Demographic
2. a What is the highest degree you received?	b. Knowledge
3. e To what extent are you excited about playing in next week's game?	c. Behavior
4. d/b What kinds of questions would you say are the most helpful for a teacher to ask during a class discussion?	d. Values/opinions
5. d What do you think about the new detention policy?	e. Feelings
6. b How old was General Johnson when he died?	f. Sensory
7. b How many credits does one need to get a degree?	

Activity 19.4:
Do Some Observational Research

In this activity, you will actually do some observational research. Go to a nearby parking lot where there are a lot of cars going in and out fairly frequently (a shopping mall lot or garage would be ideal). Observe drivers when they back out of their parking spaces. The research question for you to investigate is whether people do or do not take longer to back out of a space when someone is waiting for that space.

You are to obtain data on the time a person takes to back out when another car is waiting and when there is no car waiting. You also will obtain data on the gender of the driver and the number of passengers in the waiting car.

A simple observation sheet for you to use is given below. Use a new line for each driver you observe. You should feel free to modify this sheet if you can think of ways to improve it. Observe as many drivers as you can in a 30 minute period.

Number	Start time*	End time**	Waiting***	Gender	Type of Car
			Y/N	M/F	
			Y/N	M/F	
			Y/N	M/F	
			Y/N	M/F	
			Y/N	M/F	
			Y/N	M/F	

*Start timing when the driver opens the driver's side door.
**Stop timing when the front bumper clears the parking space.
***A car is waiting if someone is waiting for the spot and the driver notices (turns toward) the waiting car before opening his or her car door.

After you have collected all of your data, record your results using an expanded copy of the form above.

Average time to back out when car is waiting _____
      When driver is female _____
      When driver is male _____

Average time to back out when car is not waiting _____
      When driver is female _____
      When driver is male _____

What do you conclude with regard to the research question?

_____
_____
_____
_____

CHAPTER 20: Content Analysis

Activity 20.1:
Content Analysis Research Questions

Which of the following questions would lend themselves well to content analysis?

1. Do students like school more if taught by a teacher of the same ethnicity?

2. What sorts of techniques do tennis coaches use to increase the motivation of 12-year-olds to play tennis?

3. Is violence on television different from violence in classical drama?

4. Do boys or girls score higher on SAT examinations?

5. Are women or men portrayed more favorably in 1930s movies?

6. Are after-school detention programs effective?

7. How do the ingredients found in recipes in 1940s cookbooks compare with those found in 1990s cookbooks?

8. To what extent did capitalism develop in nineteenth-century China?

Activity 20.2:
Content Analysis Categories

What categories could be used by a researcher who wishes to do a content analysis of the following? Working with a partner, suggest some possible categories that the researcher might use in each case.

1. *Coverage of minority groups in social studies textbooks*

   Possible categories might include:

   _____

   _____

2. *How characters are portrayed in Saturday morning television cartoon programs*

   Possible categories might include:

   _____

   _____

3. *Issues discussed in newspaper editorials*

   Possible categories might include:

   _____

   _____

4. *Themes used in magazine advertisements*

   Possible categories might include:

   _____

   _____

5. *Emotions presented in popular songs*

   Possible categories might include:

   _____

   _____

Activity 20.3:
Advantages vs. Disadvantages of Content Analysis

In the space provided in front of each of the statements listed below, write "T" if the statement is true. Write "F" if the statement is false.

1. _____ Content analysis deals mainly with recorded information.

2. _____ Content analysis is unobtrusive.

3. _____ Content analysis is strongly influenced by the researcher's presence.

4. _____ Content analysis cannot be done with songs.

5. _____ Content analysis is extremely difficult to do.

6. _____ Content analysis is relatively economical compared to other research methodologies.

7. _____ Content analysis data is primarily in the form of numbers.

8. _____ The information needed to do a content analysis usually is readily available.

9. _____ It is fairly easy to establish validity in content analysis.

10. _____ Content analysis requires extensive training before one can undertake it.

Activity 20.4:
Do a Content Analysis

In this activity, you will actually do a content analysis.

A professor at a large Midwestern university is trying to decide what to do in a class entitled "Values of American Society," which she has recently been asked to teach. One of her colleagues suggests that one way to approach the subject is to ask her students to do a content analysis of advertisements taken from various national magazines and newspapers.

The following is a sample of three advertisements that she collects. Read these over carefully. Then ask yourself what societal values are reflected in these advertisements. Decide on a few categories and tally how often each value is represented in this sample of ads. What conclusions can you suggest based on your content analysis of this brief sample?

HAVE YOU SEEN THE NEW ROVER?

What a beauty! Undreamed of power (until now) is provided by the newly designed V-8 engine with extra oomph! Several new safety features enhance your security. And sound! Wow! You have to listen to a symphony on the CD player. A real-life concert never sounded this good. Visit your dealer today for a demonstration!!

HAD YOUR PICTURE TAKEN LATELY?

Our cameras are the best in the business -- unmatched for fidelity, ease of use, and reliability. If you want to take exceptional pictures with ease, get one today. You won't be sorry!
(P.S. Tell them Jake sent you.)

WE'VE GOT IT!
NO MATTER WHAT YOU ARE LOOKING FOR ON THE INTERNET, WE'VE GOT IT. CHECK OUR WEBSITE AT WWW.INERNET.COM

CHAPTER 21: Ethnographic Research

Activity 21.1: Ethnographic Research Questions

Activity 21.2: True or False?

Activity 21.3: Do Some Ethnographic Research

Activity 21.1:
Ethnographic Research Questions

Which of the following questions would lend themselves well to ethnographic research?

1. Which do students like better, filmstrips or movies about the same topic?

2. What is the social structure of children attending nursery school?

3. How do beginning counselors interact with teachers?

4. Is client-centered therapy more effective than traditional therapy with teenagers?

5. How do middle school teachers plan their daily routine?

6. What is the status of social studies supervision in our state?

7. How are women portrayed in popular television shows?

8. In what ways do the questions parents and teachers ask children differ?

Activity 21.2:
True or False?

Write "T" in the space provided in front of each of the statements listed below that are true. Write "F" in front of each statement that is false.

1. _____ There is no experimental "treatment" in ethnographic research.

2. _____ Participant observation is not used in ethnographic research.

3. _____ Ethnographic researchers usually begin their research with precise hypotheses.

4. _____ A particular strength of ethnographic research is that it can reveal nuances and subtleties that other methodologies may miss.

5. _____ Ethnographic research is particularly suitable for topics that defy simple quantification.

6. _____ Most ethnographic studies are done in laboratory settings.

7. _____ The samples studied by ethnographers are usually quite small.

8. _____ A major advantage of ethnographic research is that it provides the researcher with a much more comprehensive perspective than do other forms of educational research.

9. _____ Ethnographic research is highly dependent on the particular researcher's observations.

10. _____ A major check on the accuracy of an ethnographer's observations lies in the quality of his or her field notes.

11. _____ Ethnographic data are usually collected in the form of numbers.

Activity 21.3:
Do Some Ethnographic Research

In this activity, you are to observe a class session or other group meeting of one kind or another. Take careful field notes in which you try to record *everything* important that occurs. Immediately afterwards, write up a field diary of your observations. Describe your conclusions below. What problems, if any, did you encounter?

Conclusions:

_____

_____

_____

_____

_____

_____

_____

_____

_____

_____

Problems:

_____

_____

_____

_____

_____

_____

_____

_____

_____

_____

CHAPTER 22: Historical Research

Activity 22.1:
Historical Research Questions

Which of the following questions would lend themselves well to historical research?

1. What was life like for a woman teacher in the 1920s?

2. What sorts of techniques do speech teachers use to improve an individual's ability to give an extemporaneous speech?

3. How do art teachers teach drawing to primary school children?

4. Is client-centered therapy more effective with teenagers than traditional therapy?

5. What were the beginnings of the modern social studies?

6. Is the deception of research subjects ever seen as appropriate by students?

7. How were women portrayed in 1930s fiction?

8. When should children be enrolled in swimming classes?

9. How has the age of children leaving home changed between the years 1920 and 1980?

Activity 22.2:
Primary or Secondary Source?

In the space provided after each of the items listed below, write "P" if the item is a primary historical source or "S" if it is a secondary source.

1. An essay written by an eighth grader in 1935 _____

2. A 1945 photograph of a high school cheerleading squad _____

3. A magazine article describing a school board meeting in 1920 _____

4. A World War II veteran's description of an air raid _____

5. A history textbook _____

6. A description of a scientific experiment carried out by one of the authors of this textbook _____

7. A complete set of the *Encyclopedia Britannica* for years 1949-1953 _____

8. Music charts composed for use by the Benny Goodman sextet in the 1930s _____

9. A newspaper editorial commenting on the death of John F. Kennedy _____

Activity 22.3:
What Kind of Historical Source?

Match the historical source listed in Column B with the appropriate example in Column A.

Column A: Examples	Column B: Kind of Historical Source
1. _____ A 1994 high school yearbook	a. Document
2. _____ A table found in an eighteenth-century colonial home	b. numerical record
	c. oral statement
3. _____ A baseball cap worn by Babe Ruth in the 1930s	d. relic
4. _____ A copy of the Ph.D. dissertation of one of the authors of this text	
5. _____ A letter written by the wife of Henry Kissinger	
6. _____ A cartoon from a copy of a 1940s issue of *Time* magazine	
7. _____ The diary of a nineteenth-century schoolmarm in rural Kentucky	
8. _____ A copy of the year 2000 census report	
9. _____ A school budget from a large urban high school district for the year 1984	
10. _____ A recorded interview with folksinger Joan Baez	

Activity 22.4:
True or False?

Write "T" in the space provided in front of each of the statements listed below that are true. Write "F" in front of each statement that is false.

1. _____ A major advantage of historical research is that it permits the study of certain kinds of topics and questions that can be studied in no other way.

2. _____ *Internal criticism* in historical research refers to the genuineness of the documents that the researcher uses.

3. _____ A *primary source* is a document prepared by an individual who was not a direct witness to an event.

4. _____ A disadvantage of historical research is that the measures used to control for internal validity in other kinds of research are not available in a historical study.

5. _____ It would be difficult to draw a representative sample of data when doing a historical study.

6. _____ Many historical studies are done in libraries.

7. _____ It would be unusual to find a hypothesis in a historical study.

8. _____ There is no manipulation of variables in historical research.

9. _____ "How were young women educated in nineteenth-century convent schools?" would be an example of a question investigated through historical research.

10. _____ "When was that document written?" is one example of a question that involved *external criticism.*

11. _____ The reading and summarization of historical data is rarely a neat, orderly sequence of steps to be followed.

Chapter 23: Mixed-Methods Research

Activity 23.1:
Mixed-Methods Research Questions

Which of the questions would lend themselves well to mixed-methods research?

1. What is the relationship between science achievement scores and reading achievement scores among sixth-graders?

2. Are homeless children more likely to be depressed, as assessed by depression inventories and analysis of their diaries?

3. What are the important variables that lead to substance abuse among pre-teens, and are these variables related to one another?

4. What are the lived experiences of child prodigies in the field of music?

5. What distinct groupings of parents are revealed by demographic data (e.g., age, education, income, and number of children in the family), and how are these groups qualitatively different from one another?

6. Can cooperative learning improve the performance of fourth-graders on standardized mathematics tests, compared to a comparison group undergoing traditional instruction?

Activity 23.2:
Identifying Mixed-Methods Designs

Identify each of the following mixed-methods studies as one of the following:

      (a)   Exploratory Design
      (b)   Explanatory Design
      (c)   Triangulation Design

1. _____ A researcher is interested in studying the relationship between junk food consumption and school grades. She has students fill out a questionnaire that asks which junk foods people eat and how much they eat. This yields an overall "junk food score." She correlates this score with student grades in math, science, English, and history. She then conducts interviews with individual students to find out: (a) if there may be differences in the correlations with junk food consumption across the different subject areas, and (b) whether there are other factors (e.g., student exercise) that mitigate the potential negative effects of junk food consumption.

2. _____ A psychologist wants to study the effects of bullying on student self-esteem and school violence. She asks each of 32 teachers to nominate two students: one who is often bullied, and one who is never bullied. She administers a self-esteem inventory to each student. She also checks school records to discover how many times each student has received referrals to the front office for aggressive behavior. The non-bullied and bullied groups are then compared on these variables. A subgroup of six students from each category is also shown a picture of two students in a fight. They are then asked to write an essay about what causes the fight, and whether either of the students was "justified" in fighting. These essays are then subjected to content analysis in an attempt to determine whether one group finds violence more acceptable than the other.

3. _____ An educator wishes to understand the important components of student satisfaction with online courses. He holds focus groups with students currently enrolled in online courses and identifies three variables that seem important to student satisfaction: (a) sufficient technical support for dealing with computer problems; (b) clear expectations for student performance at the start of the course; and (c) fast feedback (less than three days) on student assignments and tests. Using these results, he constructs a measure that has five questions measuring each of the three variables. The next semester, he administers this measure to 500 students enrolled in online courses, and correlates scores on the three variables with course evaluations. These results help validate his earlier qualitative findings.

Activity 23.3:
Research Questions in Mixed-Methods Designs

When designing a mixed-methods research study, it is helpful to have both quantitative and qualitative research questions. These questions not only demonstrate that the study is truly a mixed-methods design, but also help to guide analysis of the data that has been collected during the study. Which of the follow questions cover both quantitative and qualitative issues?

1. What do teachers in large cities think about school security? Is it different in small cities?

2. How do rural parents see the educational needs of their children? Is this related to income and educational level?

3. How much verbal violence is shown in family interaction? Is the amount related to the extent of television viewing?

4. Is the amount of family time together related to academic success, and does counseling affect both?

Activity 23.4:
Identifying Terms in Mixed-Methods Studies

Match the following terms with their corresponding definitions:

(a) Quantizing
(b) Qualitizing
(c) Internal Validity
(d) Generalizability
(e) Credibility
(f) Transferability

1. _____ A term from quantitative research that corresponds to the soundness of a study's design. When this is high, there are no alternative explanations for the findings – the only explanation is the manipulation created by the experimenter.

2. _____ The conversion of quantitative data into qualitative data.

3. _____ A term from qualitative research that corresponds to how justified it is to apply the results of the current study in a new situation of environment.

4. _____ A term from quantitative research that describes the extent to which the results of a given study will apply across changes in situations or participants.

5. _____ The conversion of qualitative data into quantitative data.

6. _____ A term from qualitative research that refers to the soundness of a study's conclusions. When this is high, we believe the researcher's interpretation of his or her results.

CHAPTER 24: Action Research

Activity 24.1: Action Research Questions

Activity 24.2: True or False?

Activity 24.1:
Action Research Questions

Which of the following questions might lend themselves well to action research?

1. Do students learn more from older or younger children?

2. Is the content found in the literature anthologies in our district biased, and if so, how?

3. Would filmstrips help our elementary teachers teach multiplication to third-graders?

4. Is phonics more effective than look-say as a method of teaching reading?

5. What kinds of things do music teachers do as they go about their daily routine?

6. How might we improve the quality of our school's social studies program?

7. Is the use of detention successful with elementary school students?

8. What are the effects of giving students with serious behavior problems choices about how to behave in class?

9. What has been the effect of federal legislation on school reform at the district level?

Activity 24.2:
True or False?

In the space provided in front of each statement below, write "T" if the statement is true. Write "F" if the statement is false.

1. _____ Action research is research conducted so that a decision can be reached about an issue of concern at the local school level.

2. _____ Administrators would rarely participate in action research.

3. _____ Those involved in action research generally want to solve some day-to-day immediate problem.

4. _____ One advantage of action research is that it is not limited to generalizability.

5. _____ Action research requires mastery of at least one of the major types of educational research.

6. _____ An assumption underlying action research is that those who work in schools want to engage, at least to some degree, in some form of systematic research.

7. _____ An important aspect of participatory action research is that the question or problem being investigated is one that is of interest to all the parties involved.

8. _____ It is not unusual in much action research to find the use of more than one instrument.

9. _____ The researcher is the key instrument in action research studies.

10. _____ A key characteristic of most action research is that the data collection methods are chosen by the stakeholders.

11. _____ Action research can be done by teachers.

12. _____ Unfortunately, action research cannot help teachers to identify problems and issues systematically.

CHAPTER 25: Preparing Research Proposals and Reports

Activity 25.1: Put Them in Order

Activity 25.1:
Put Them in Order

Listed below are many of the major sections of a research report, but they are out of order. Rearrange them into the proper order.

1. Description of the sample

2. Suggestions for further research

3. Purpose of the study

4. Table of contents

5. Definition of terms

6. Description of findings

7. Justification of the study

8. Description of the methods of data analysis used

9. Description of the research design

10. Research question

11. Review of related literature

12. Description of the instruments used

13. Discussion of internal validity

14. Detailed explanation of the procedures followed

15. Discussion of findings and conclusions

AUTHORS' SUGGESTED ANSWERS TO ODD-NUMBERED QUESTIONS

Please consult your instructor for answers to the even-numbered questions.

PROBLEM SHEETS

Chapter 1: The Nature of Research

Activity 1.1: Empirical vs. Nonempirical Research

1. Empirical
3. Nonempirical
5. Nonempirical

Activity 1.2: Basic vs. Applied Research

1. Basic
3. Basic
5. Applied

Activity 1.3: Types of Research

1. g
3. c
5. f
7. h

Activity 1.4: Assumptions

Many answers are possible. Here are ours.

1. One assumption here is that punishment is necessary to ensure "good" behavior on the part of children.
3. An assumption is that a small amount of effort now will save one having to do a large amount later.
5. An assumption here is that taking algebra with Mrs. West is going to be unpleasant.

Activity 1.5: General Research Types: Authors' Suggested Answers

1. Associational
3. Intervention
5. Descriptive
7. Intervention

Chapter 2: The Research Problem

Activity 2.1: Research Questions and Related Designs

1. survey
3. survey

5. case study
7. content analysis

Activity 2.2: Changing General Topics into Research Questions

A variety of possibilities exist. Here are a few.

1. Is class size related to student achievement?
3. What factors are related to text anxiety among students?
5. How does the amount of alcohol consumption on New Year's Eve compare with that consumed on Super Bowl Sunday?
7. Which style of counseling -- client-centered of behavioral therapy -- is more effective?
9. What were the chief characteristics of the charter school movement in the twentieth century?

Activity 2.3: Operational Definitions

1. not operational
3. operational
5. operational
7. not operational
9. operational

Activity 2.4: Justification

1 is the stronger justification, not because it is longer but because it gives a number of reasons as to why the author thinks the study is important.

Chapter 3: Variables and Hypotheses

Activity 3.1: Directional vs. Non-Directional Hypotheses

1. D
3. D
5. ND

Activity 3.2: Testing Hypotheses

1. Quality of professor is related to amount (or degree) of interest in students.
3. Gender is related to level of management position to which appointed.

There are many possible restatements. Here are a few.

1. Professors who receive high ratings from students (a 4 or 5 on a 1-5 rating scale where 5 is high and 1 is low) spend more than two hours per week in their offices and never miss holding office hours.
3. There are no women CEOs in any of the 500 companies listed this year in *Fortune* magazine.

Activity 3.3: Categorical vs. Quantitative Variables

1. CV
3. CV
5. QV
7. QV

Activity 3.4: Independent and Dependent Variables

1. Independent variable = seeing vs. not seeing the film
   Dependent variable = attitudes toward sharing candy
   Constant: grade level

5. Independent variable = presence of computers vs. no computers
   Dependent variable = student achievement
   Constant: grade level

Activity 3.6: Moderator Variables

1. IV is method of teaching
   DV is amount of chemistry learned
   ModV might be gender of students

3. IV is amount of time spent studying
   DV is grades received
   ModV might be subject studied

5. IV is fiction/non-fiction
   DV is strength of preference
   ModV might be subject of fiction/non-fiction

Chapter 4: Ethics and Research

Activity 4.1: Ethical or Not?

1. Yes; it is unethical to require students to participate in a study without their consent.
3. This study violated practically every ethical standard there is -- from informed consent to deception to imposing physical harm on the participants.

Activity 4.2: Some Ethical Dilemmas

1. The question at issue here is whether deception is ever justified. Most researchers would agree that if deception involves some risk to others, it is unethical. Some feel if there is no risk to the participants in a study, as is indicated here, deceiving subjects is not unethical. Some researchers point out that it is impossible to study some things, such as that of patients in hospitals, without deceiving them. Others argue that casual observation is not unethical, but that it is unethical to violate a person's privacy deliberately (e.g., through the use of binoculars). And some say that deception is never justified.

3. Opinions differ here, but in my opinion, all of this information should be given to potential subjects in clinical trials.

Activity 4.3: Some Violations of Ethical Practice

1. f
3. e
5. c

Activity 4.4: Why Would These Research Practices be Unethical?

1. "We are required to ask you to sign this consent form. You needn't read it; it's just routine." *Participants are being asked, in effect, to give their consent without being informed of what the study is about (and accordingly of any risks they might incur).*

3. "Yes, as a student at this university you are required to participate in this study." *No one (especially students) is ever required to participate in a study.*

5. "Requiring students to participate in class discussions might be harmful to some, but it is necessary for our research." *No participant in a study should be exposed to any sort of harm, physical or psychological, unless they are aware of such harm and are willing to undergo the risk involved.*

Activity 4.5: Is It Ethical to Use Prisoners as Subjects?

1. Many answers are possible here, and students should be encouraged to offer their suggestions. Here is some food for thought: The Center for Bioethics at the University of Minnesota advocates using inmates only when the research could benefit prisoners as individuals or as a group. Prisoner advocacy groups point that not all prisoners involved in research have been unwitting or unwilling participants. A spokesperson for the American Civil Liberties Union has indicated that the position of the ACLU is that prisoners should not be excluded from trials that are efficacious, that are going to improve their health or that they would normally have access to if they were members of the community. On the other hand, the ACLU does not want prisoners to be used as guinea pigs for trials that companies would not complete in the community.

Chapter 5: Locating and Reviewing the Literature

Activity 5.2: Where Would You Look?

1. *Review of Educational Research*
3. The current issue of *Books in Print* (to locate some books that might discuss research on the topic)
5. *Dissertation Abstracts*
7. A textbook in educational sociology

Chapter 6: Sampling

Activity 6.1: Identifying Types of Sampling

1. b
3. g
5. d
7. f
9. g

Activity 6.2: Drawing a Random Sample

The results of this exercise will depend on which line in the Table of Random Numbers you decide to use. You should find, however, that as your sample size increases, the characteristics of your sample will approach (and in some cases match) the characteristics of the population. I include an example for sample of 10 below, using the first line from the random numbers table.

Student Number	Gender	School	IQ
83	F	Cortez	104
57	M	Beals	101
95	F	Cortez	95
29	M	Adams	96
78	F	Cortez	111
49	M	Beals	111
37	F	Beals	128
20	F	Adams	104
15	M	Adams	109
77	M	Cortez	111

Averages						
N = 10	M	F	A	B	C	IQ
Average	.5	.5	.3	.3	.4	98
Population	.49	.51	.33	.31	.36	109.8

Notice that my sample is actually quite similar to the population in most respects, except that it has a markedly lower IQ average. Were I to enlarge the size of my sample, the chances are that the IQ average would increase. Can you see why?

Activity 6.3: When is it Appropriate to Generalize?

1. No, it would not. Because only *unsuccessful* hijackers are included in the sample.

Activity 6.4: True or False?

1. T
3. T
5. T
7. T
9. F

Activity 6.5: Stratified Sampling

The strata to be used are school level and (possibly) gender of the administrators.

Chapter 7: Instrumentation

Activity 7.1: Major Categories of Instruments and Their Uses

1. g
2. d
3. b

Activity 7.2: Which Type of Instrument is Most Appropriate?

1. Q
3. I
5. RS
7. I
9. TS
11. RS
13. Q
15. TS

Activity 7.3: Types of Scales

1. d
3. b
5. d
7. c
9. c

Activity 7.4: Norm-Referenced vs. Criterion-Referenced Instruments

1. C
3. N
5. N
7. N
9. N

Activity 7.5: Developing a Rating Scale

Only a few of the indicators that were originally developed were converted directly into the rating scale. All of the items except #2 and #11 relate directly to one or more indicators. For example, item #1 encompasses two indicators: "Are students free to move outside without an adult present?" and "Can students leave the classroom on their own, or must they request permission?" Note that in most cases the wording of the indicator has been changed in the transition.

Items #2 and #11 do not relate to specific indicators, but rather emerged during the conversion process. A decision by this student to focus on items that can be directly observed did cause her to eliminate many indicators, particularly those under the headings of curriculum and parental participation.

Rating scales can be substantially improved by giving explicit descriptions of each point on the scale, as in the following example for Item #1:

1. Students are observed to move around without teacher permission

1	2	3	4	5
(Never)	(Less than 11)	(11-30 Instance)	(31-50 instances)	(More than 50 instances)

Chapter 8: Validity and Reliability

Activity 8.1: Instrument Validity

Many answers can be given here. Here are some possibilities:

1. To measure the degree to which a person enjoys modern art, you might:
    *   use a rating scale to have a person rate (on a scale of 1-low, to 5-high) various types of paintings (modern and other)
    *   interview a person in depth about his or her feelings about modern art

3. To measure the attitudes of local residents toward the building of a new ballpark in downtown San Francisco, you might:

- mail out a questionnaire to a randomly selected sample of residents in which you ask them to respond to questions about the building of the ballpark
- interview a random sample of residents questions concerning their feelings about the building of the ballpark

Activity 8.2: Instrument Reliability (1)

These data indicate that the test is reliable. With few exceptions, students performed similarly on both administrations of the test. Later (in Chapter 10), we discuss a better way to analyze such data.

Activity 8.3: Instrument Reliability (2)

1. c
3. a
5. b

Activity 8.4: What Kind of Evidence?

1. Criterion-related
3. Content-related
5. Criterion-related

Activity 8.5: What Constitutes Construct-Related Evidence of Validity?

1. Many possibilities will suggest themselves. Here are a few of ours. In an attempt to establish construct validity for the paper and pencil test of honesty he or she is developing, the researcher might compare scores on his or her test with:
   - *ratings* by employers testifying to an individual's behavior in the workplace.
   - *whether*, when given an opportunity to lie or steal something of value, an individual is observed refusing to do so.
   - *statements* by teachers or friends as to the degree of honesty an individual displays
   - *scores* of a group of convicted felons on the test.

Chapter 9: Internal Validity

Activity 9.1: Threats to Internal Validity

1. *Mortality.* If the students who dropped out had a greater decrease in achievement motivation than those who remained, their loss will affect the male group more than the female group. The remaining male group will appear to have less of a decline in motivation than is really the case for the whole group.

3. *Regression.* Since all of the students who took the second test were excellent students to begin with, their lower average score on the test two weeks later may be due to the fact that their scores regressed downward toward the mean.
5. *Maturation.* The students are eight months older.

Activity 9.2: Which Type of Threat?

1. h
2. g
3. a
4. b
5. c
6. d

Activity 9.3: Controlling Threats to Internal Validity

1. *Instrument decay.* Either standardize the instrumentation process, or schedule data collection times so that the data collector does not get fatigued.
2. *Loss of subjects (mortality).* This is the most difficult of all threats to control. The best way, of course, is to do one's best to ensure subjects do not drop out of the study. If possible, one may be able to argue that those who dropped out were not significantly different from those who remained.
3. *Location.* Keep the location constant.
4. *Implementation.* In an intervention-type methods study, have each method taught by all the teachers in the study. Or, if possible, provide detailed training and observe the implementers to ensure they do not differ on some pertinent characteristic.

Chapter 10: Descriptive Statistics

Activity 10.1: Construct a Frequency Polygon

The lecture group performed, overall, at a lower level than the inquiry group. A greater number of students in the lecture group scored toward the low end of the distribution of scores. Fewer scored toward the high end. The difference can be illustrated further. For example, we find 25 cases above a score of 22 in the inquiry group compared with only 13 cases above that score in the lecture group. There are 23 cases below a score of 17 in the lecture group, compared with 14 cases in the inquiry group. The curve for the lecture group is more symmetrical, whereas the inquiry curve has a few cases at the low end of the scale. As you can see, frequency polygons are of considerable help in communicating all of the information contained in a group of scores.

Your completed frequency polygon should look like the one shown here.

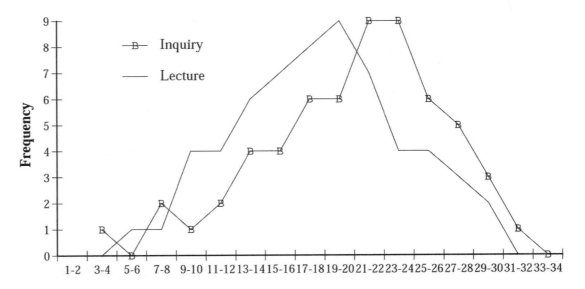

Activity 10.2: Comparing Frequency Polygons

1. Experimental (Curriculum) group = **5** percent; Comparison group = **3** percent.
3. We would say yes because the curriculum group had more cases of high scores (e.g., 32 percent vs. 14 percent above a score of 15), and fewer scores in the middle (e.g., 57 percent vs. 71 percent between scores of 8 and 14).

Activity 10.3: Calculating Averages

1. The mean = **20.5**
3. The mean for Set A = **51**, and the median = **50**

We see that the means and the medians are identical. However, the scores in Set B are much more spread out. This is confirmed once we find the range, the difference between the highest and lowest scores in each set. For Set A, the range is **15** points. For Set B, the range is **94** points!

Activity 10.4: Calculating the Standard Deviation

The standard deviation for this set is 14.08.

Activity 10.5: Calculating a Correlation Coefficient

1. 135 (6) = 810
3. 810 − 720 = 90
5. $24^2 = 576$
7. 172 (6) = 1032
9. 1032 − 900 = 132
11. Square root of 14,256 = 119.4
12. 90/119.4 = <u>.75</u>   This is a substantial correlation, indicating that students with more pencils also have more pens. Surprise!

Activity 10.6: Analyzing Crossbreak Tables

1. Most of the counselors who used a Gestalt approach received their training at Happy Valley State, with College of the Specific a respectable second. Most of those who used a behavior modification approach received their training at Multiversity II, followed by Happy Valley State. Most of those who used a Rogerian approach were trained at College of the Specific.

Activity 10.7: Comparing z Scores

1. James, as he scored two standard deviations above the mean in his group, while Felicia scored only one standard deviation above the mean in her group.
3. a. raw score = **55**
   b. raw score = **120**
   c. raw score = **80**

Activity 10.10: Comparing Scores

1. This cannot be determined, as the subject matter is not comparable.
3. They should most likely not receive the same letter grade if based on just these scores. A 77 in Biology is ½ standard deviation *below* the mean of Biology scores, while a 77 in statistics is one standard deviation *above* the mean of statistics scores.
5. Student "C" is noteworthy for scoring two standard deviations above the mean in History, one standard deviation above the mean in Statistics, yet one and one-half standard deviations *below* the mean in Biology.

Activity 10.11: Custodial Times

Gus is the only custodian who did poorly on three or more (actually four) tasks.

Chapter 11: Inferential Statistics

Activity 11.1: Probability

Since the probability of getting four heads on any given sample is only .06, this outcome for the first sample would lead me to tentatively accept the hypothesis that the coin is dishonest. Any other outcome would clearly not support the hypothesis.

The procedure you followed in this exercise is essentially that used in deriving probabilities in any statistical inference test. This is, the outcome from a particular sample is compared to a distribution of possible outcomes and its probability is determined.

Researchers generally take certain probabilities as indicative of a nonchance relationship. If the probability of obtaining a particular result (outcome, relationship) is less than .05 (one chance in 20), it is customary to take it as *statistically significant* or probably *not due to chance*). Clearly, if the probability is less than 5 percent (e.g., 1 percent), we are more confident that we are not simply dealing with chance. These values (1 percent and 5 percent) are frequently spoken of as *levels of significance.*

Consequently, when a research report states that a particular relationship was significant at the .05 level, it means that the chance of the finding being simply a fluke, due to the particular sample that was used, was less than 5 in 100. It means that the result (outcome, relationship) is worth noting and tentatively acceptable as a reproducible relationship for a specified population. Note, however, as we mentioned in the text (see p. 000) that statistical significance is not the same thing as practical significance. A correlation of .23, for example, can under certain circumstances be statistically significant. However, it is usually too low to be of practical use.

Activity 11.2: Learning to Read a *t*-Table

A sample with **10 d.f.** would require a *t*-value of **2.764** to be statistically significant at the **.01** level.

A sample with **25 d.f.** would require a *t*-value of **1.708** to be considered statistically significant at the **.05** level; to be statistically significant at the **.01** level would require a *t*-value of **2.485**.

Activity 11.3: Calculate a *t*-test

	Inquiry Group	Lecture Group
Mean	87	85
Standard deviation (SD)	2	3
Standard error of the mean (SEM)	0.4	0.6
Standard error of the difference (SED)	.72	

SEM$_{inquiry}$ = 2/5 = 0.4   **SEM$_{lecture}$ = 3/5 = 0.6**

SED = sq. root of **$(0.4)^2$ + $(0.6)^2$** = sq. root of **(.16 + .36)** = sq. root of **.52 = .72**

$t = \dfrac{\text{Mean}_{inquiry} - \text{Mean}_{lecture}}{SED}$ = **87 − 85/.72 = 2/.72 = 2.78**

Degrees of freedom (df) = (n_1) + (n_2) = **(26 + 26) - 2 = 50.** Thus the result (the difference in means) of **2** points is statistically significant at the **.01** level (indicating it is a real difference, and not just a fluke due to chance). It is doubtful, however, that a difference of only **2** points would be considered practically significant.

Activity 11.4: Perform a Chi-Square Test

Table 11.4

University	Number of Students Enrolling in Physical Education Courses	Number of Students Participating in Intramural Sports	Totals
Alpha	70 (60)	30 (40)	100
Beta	130 (120)	70 (80)	200
Kappa	160 (180)	140 (120)	300
Totals	360	240	600

$(70 - 60)^2/60 = 10^2/60 = 100/60 = 1.67$
$(30 - 40)^2/40 = -10^2/40 = 100/40 = 2.50$
$(130 - 120)^2/120 = 10^2/120 = 100/120 = 0.83$
$(70 - 80)^2/80 = -10^2/80 = 100/80 = 1.25$
$(160 - 180)^2/180 = -20^2/180 = 400/180 = 2.22$
$(140 - 120)^2/120 = 20^2/120 = 400/120 = 3.33$
Chi-square = **11.80**

To determine the degrees of freedom (d.f.), multiply the number of rows minus one (r – 1) times the number of columns minus one (c – 1). In this case, it would be **(3 – 1) x (2 – 1) = 2**. The chi-square table indicates that, with two d.f., a value of **5.99** is required for a result to be statistically significant. Is the value you obtained (**11.80**) statistically significant? Yes _X_ No _____

Activity 11.5: Conduct a *T*-Test

1. Were the results statistically significant? This will depend on whether or not the results reach or exceed the proportions listed for the various degrees of freedom.
2. What basic assumption must be met to justify using a *t*-test? That the population is normally distributed on the characteristic of interest.
3. Was it met? Yes _____ No _____ Explain why it was or was not.

_____

_____

Activity 11.6: The Big Game

1. It is very unlikely Bobby could get a score of 16 by just guessing, as only 2 students out of the 500 who have taken this test received a score of 16 or better (.04%).

Chapter 12: Statistics in Perspective

Activity 12.1: Statistical vs. Practical Significance

1. Anything that can occur by chance 20 times out of 100 (a 20% chance of occurring just by chance) is not statistically significant. Whether the result is practically significant cannot be determined by its statistical significance.
3. Even though the decrease is only 3 percent, most people in the medical profession would likely say this would be important -- be practically significant.
5. This would not be. Being able to tie one's shoes three weeks earlier than other five-year-olds would make little difference to most (all?) parents.

Activity 12.2: Appropriate Techniques

1. c
3. f
5. i
7. b

Activity 12.3: Interpret the Data in Activity 11.5:

1. This will depend on the size of the difference. It is probably going to be slight since it was randomly selected in the first place.
3. Delta (Effective size).

Chapter 13: Experimental Research

Activity 13.1: Group Experimental Research Questions

1. No
3. Yes
5. No
7. Yes
9. No

Activity 13.2: Designing an Experiment

1. Because they would have no idea whether or not it was the new drug that produced any results.
3. No. They might react differently than if they did not know which drug they were getting.

Activity 13.3: Characteristics of Experimental Research

1. i
3. b
5. f
7. c

Activity 13.4: Random Selection Versus Random Assignment

1. RA
3. RS

Note that numbers 3 and 4 are not experiments.

Chapter 14: Single-Subject Research

Activity 14.1: Single-Subject Research Questions

1. No
3. No
5. Yes
7. No

Activity 14.2: Characteristics of Single-Subject Research

1. b
3. c
5. g
7. f

Activity 14.3: Analyze Some Single-Subject Data

The treatment appears to have been effective with behaviors 1 and 2 because frequencies increase after the treatment was introduced. Effectiveness with behavior 3 is unclear because frequencies increased in observations 9 and 10 before the treatment was introduced, but then increased only slightly thereafter.

Chapter 15: Correlational Research

Activity 15.1: Correlational Research Questions

1. No
3. No
5. Yes

Activity 15.2: What Kind of Correlation?

1. positive
3. positive
5. positive
7. negative
9. not

Activity 15.3: Think up an example

There are many possibilities. Here are a few.

1. strong positive: drug use and arrest record
3. weak positive: liking for mystery novels and liking for adventure novels
5. little or none: eating carrots and reading ability

Activity 15.4: Match the Correlation Coefficient to its Scatterplot

a. $r = .90$
c. $r = -.90$
e. $r = .35$
g. $r = .-50$

Activity 15.5: Calculate a Correlation Coefficient

This would indicate a very high relationship between reading and writing for these students.

$$r = \frac{(5)(1328) - (81)(78)}{\sqrt{[(5)(1373) - (81^2)][(5)(1300) - (78^2)]}}$$

$$r = \frac{(6640) - (6318)}{\sqrt{[(6865) - (6561)][(6500) - (6084)]}}$$

$$r = \frac{322}{\sqrt{(304)(416)}} =$$

$$r = \frac{322}{\sqrt{355.6}} = .91$$

Activity 15.7: Correlation in Everyday Life

Many different relationships might be suggested. Here are ours:

1. "A fool and his money are soon parted" suggests a <u>negative</u> relationship between *foolishness* and *savings*.
3. "You can't grow grass on a busy street" suggests a <u>positive</u> relationship between *baldness* and *thoughtfulness*.
5. "What fails to destroy me makes me stronger" suggests a <u>positive</u> relationship between *non-fatal adversity* and *psychological strength*.
7. "You can't make an omelet without breaking some eggs" suggests a <u>positive</u> relationship between *progress* and *suffering*.
9. "All that glitters is not gold" suggests a <u>negative</u> relationship between *appearance* and *quality*.

Chapter 16: Causal-Comparative Research

Activity 16.1: Causal-Comparative Research Questions

1. No
3. Yes
5. No
7. No

Activity 16.2: Experiment or Causal-Comparative Study

1a. Causal-comparative
1c. Experiment
1e. Causal-comparative

Activity 16.3: Causal-Comparative Versus Experimental Hypotheses

Hypothesis #1: This hypothesis could be studied using either methodology. The experimental method would require that teachers be trained in each method and students randomly assigned to each method. The causal-comparative

Hypothesis #3: This hypothesis could be studied most appropriately by means of an experiment. Existing examples of the simulation-of-pregnancy technique, as required by the causal-comparative approach, are likely to be rare. Furthermore, the nature of the intervention is such that the more powerful experimental method could likely be used without great expense or inconvenience.

Activity 16.4: Analyze Some Causal-Comparative Data

The females do have a higher average score. The difference, however, is only three points (82.9 vs. 79.5). The importance of this can be assessed by calculating the effect size (see page 249 in the text). Causation is highly questionable due to the possible effect of such extraneous variables as age, background in mathematics, class attendance, and/or GPA. Generalizing beyond this one class is clearly inappropriate.

Chapter 17: Survey Results

Activity 17.1: Survey Research Questions

1. Yes
3. No
5. Yes
7. Yes

Activity 17.2: Types of Surveys

1. d
3. g
5. a
7. b

Activity 17.3: Open- vs. Closed-Ended Questions

There are many possible closed-ended questions that you might suggest. Here are a few:

1. Which of the following was your favorite subject when you were in elementary school?
   a. social studies
   b. reading
   c. physical education
   d. English
   e. Other

3. Which of the following factors contributed to the election of George W. Bush in 2000?
   a. money
   b. reputation as Governor of Texas
   c. personality
   d. election fraud
   e. his educational background

Chapter 18: The Nature of Qualitative Research

Activity 18.1: Qualitative Research Questions

1. No
3. Yes
5. Yes
7. No
9. Yes

Activity 18.2: Qualitative vs. Quantitative Research

1. Qualitative
3. Quantitative
5. Quantitative
7. Quantitative
9. Qualitative
11. Quantitative

Activity 18.3: Approaches to Qualitative Research

1. b
3. c
5. d
7. c

Chapter 19: Observations and Interviewing

Activity 19.1: Observer Roles

1. d
3. a
5. d

Activity 19.2: Types of Interviews

1. c
3. c
5. c
7. d

Activity 19.3: Types of Interview Questions

1. c
3. e
5. d
7. b

Chapter 20: Content Analysis Research

Activity 20.1: Content Analysis Research Questions

1. No
3. Yes
5. Yes
7. Yes

Activity 20.2: Content Analysis Categories

1. <u>Coverage of minority groups in social studies textbooks</u>. Possible categories might include *hero, victim, domestic, partner, leader, follower, etc.*
2. <u>Issues discussed in newspaper editorials</u>. Possible categories might include *crime, homelessness, the Presidency, transportation, airports, etc.*
3. <u>Emotions presented in popular songs</u>. Possible categories might include *love, dreams, loneliness, sadness, romance, mystery, etc.*

Activity 20.3: Advantages vs. Disadvantages of Content Analysis

1. T
3. F
5. F
7. F
9. F

Chapter 21: Ethnographic Research

Activity 21.1: Ethnographic Research Questions

1. No
3. Yes
5. Yes
7. No

Activity 21.2: True or False?

1. T
3. F
5. T
7. T
9. T
11. F

Activity 21.3: Do Some Ethnographic Research

I suspect that you found this to be a difficult assignment. Don't be disappointed, however, since even experienced researchers not trained in ethnography often find this difficult. Perhaps you had difficulty determining what was important and what was not. Quite likely you were unable to record everything that went on, and probably you were not always sure about what to record and what to ignore. You also probably found it difficult not to impose your own interpretations on the various events as they occurred. What do you think about this method now?

Chapter 22: Historical Research

Activity 22.1: Historical Research Questions

1. Yes
3. No
5. Yes
7. Yes
9. Yes

Activity 22.2: Primary or Secondary Source?

1. P
3. S
5. S
7. S
9. S

Activity 22.3: What Kind of Historical Source?

1. a
3. d
5. a
7. a
9. b

Activity 22.4: True or False?

1. T
3. F
5. T
7. F
9. T
11. T

Chapter 23: Mixed-Methods Research

Activity 23.1: Mixed-Methods Research Questions

1. No
3. Yes
5. Yes

Activity 23.2: Identifying Mixed-Methods Designs

1. (b) Explanatory Design
3. (a) Exploratory Design

Activity 23.3   Research Questions in Mixed-Methods Designs

1. Qualitative Only
3. Both Qualitative and Quantitative

Activity 23.4: Soundness of Design in Mixed-Methods Studies

1. (c)
3. (f)
5. (a)

Chapter 24: Action Research

Activity 24.1: Action Research Questions

1. No
3. Yes
5. No
7. Yes
9. No

24.2: True or False?

1. T
3. T
5. F
7. T
9. F
11. T

Chapter 25: Preparing Research Proposals and Reports

Activity 25.1: Put Them in Order

1. Table of contents
2. ?
3. Justification of the study
4. ?
5. Definition of terms
6. ?
7. Description of the research design
8. ?
9. Description of the instruments used
10. ?
11. Discussion of internal validity
12. ?
13. Description of findings
14. ?
15. Suggestions for further research

Problem Sheets

Problem Sheet 1: Research Method
Problem Sheet 2: The Research Question
Problem Sheet 3: The Research Hypothesis
Problem Sheet 4: Ethics and Research
Problem Sheet 5: Review of the Literature
Problem Sheet 6: Sampling Plan
Problem Sheet 7: Instrumentation
Problem Sheet 8: Instrument Validity and Reliability
Problem Sheet 9: Internal Validity
Problem Sheet 10: Descriptive Statistics
Problem Sheet 11: Inferential Statistics
Problem Sheet 12: Statistics in Perspective
Problem Sheet 13: Research Methodology

Problem Sheet 1: Research Method

1. A possible topic or problem I am thinking of researching is:

    _____
    _____
    _____
    _____
    _____
    _____
    _____

2. The specific method that seems most appropriate for me to use at this time is (circle <u>one</u>, or if planning a mixed-methods study, circle <u>both</u> types of methods you plan to use):

    a. An experiment

    b. A survey using a written questionnaire

    c. A survey using interviews of several people

    d. A correlational study

    e. A causal-comparative study

    f. An ethnography

    g. A case study

    h. A content analysis

    i. A historical study

    j. An action research study

    k. A mixed-methods study

3. What questions (if any) might a critical researcher raise with regard to your study?

    _____
    _____
    _____
    _____
    _____
    _____
    _____

Problem Sheet 2: The Research Question

1. My (restated) research problem is:

   _____

   _____

2. My research question is:

   _____

   _____

3. Following are the key terms in the problem or question that are not clear and thus need to be defined:

   a. _____

   b. _____

   c. _____

   d. _____

   e. _____

   f. _____

4. Here are my constitutive definitions of these terms:

   _____

   _____

   _____

   _____

5. Here are my operational definitions of these terms:

   _____

   _____

   _____

   _____

6. My justification for investigating this question/problem (why I would argue that it is an important question to investigate) is as follows:

   _____

   _____

   _____

   _____

   _____

Problem Sheet 3: The Research Hypothesis

1. My research question is: _____

    _____

    _____

2.   My hypothesis is: _____

    _____

    _____

    _____

3. This hypothesis suggests a relationship between at least two variables.

    They are _____ and _____

4. More specifically, the variables in my study are:

    a. Dependent _____
    b. Independent _____

5. The dependent variable is (check one) categorical _____ quantitative_____

    The independent variable is (check one) categorical _____ quantitative_____

6. Possible extraneous variables that might affect my results include:

    a. _____
    b. _____
    c. _____
    d. _____
    e. _____

Problem Sheet 4: Ethics and Research

1. My research question is: _____

   _____

   _____

2. The possibilities for harm to participants (if any) are as follows: _____

   _____

   _____

   I would handle these problems as follows: _____

   _____

   _____

3. The possibilities of problems of confidentiality (if any) are as follows: _____

   _____

   _____

   _____

   I would handle these problems as follows: _____

   _____

   _____

4. The possibilities of problems of deception (if any) are as follows: _____

   _____

   _____

   _____

   I would handle these problems as follows: _____

   _____

   _____

5. If you think your proposed study would fit the guidelines for exempt status, state why.

   _____

   _____

   _____

Problem Sheet 5: Review of the Literature

1. The question of hypothesis in my study is: _____
   _____
   _____

2. The general reference(s) I consulted was (were): _____
   _____
   _____

3. The database I used in my search was: _____
   _____
   _____

4. The descriptors (search terms) I used were (list single descriptors and combinations in the order in which you did your search):
   _____
   _____
   _____
   _____

5. The results of my search using these descriptors were as follows:

Search #	Descriptor(s)	Results

6. Attached is a printout of my search (attach to the back of this sheet.)

7. The title of one of the abstracts located using the descriptors identified above is: (Attach a copy of the abstract.)
   _____

8. The titles of the studies I read were (note cards are attached):
   a. _____
   b. _____
   c. _____

Problem Sheet 6: Sampling Plan

1. My intended sample (subjects who would participate in my study) consists of *(tell who and how many)*: _____
    _____
    _____

2. Demographics (characteristics of the sample) are as follows:

    a. Age range _____

    b. Sex distribution _____

    c. Ethnic breakdown _____

    d. Location (where are these subjects?) _____

    e. Other characteristics not mentioned above that you deem important *(use a sheet of paper if you need more space)* _____
        _____
        _____

3. Type of sample: simple random _____ stratified random _____ systematic _____

    cluster random _____ two-stage random _____ convenience _____

    purposive _____

4. I will obtain my sample by: _____
    _____
    _____

5. External validity (I will generalize to the following population):

    a. To what accessible population?_____

    b. To what target population?_____

    c. If results are not generalizable, why not?_____

6. Ecological validity (I will generalize to the following settings/conditions):

    a. To what accessible population?_____

    b. To what target population?_____

    c. If results are not generalizable, why not?_____

Problem Sheet 7: Instrumentation

1. The question or hypothesis in my study is: _____
   _____

2. The types of instruments I plan to use are: _____
   _____

3. If I need to develop an instrument, here are two examples of the kind of questions I would ask (or tasks I would have students perform) as part of my instrument:

   a. _____

   b. _____

4. These are the existing instruments I plan to use:_____
   _____

5. The independent variable in my study is: _____

   I would describe it as follows *(circle the term in each set that applies)*:

   [quantitative or categorical] [nominal or ordinal or interval or ratio]

6. The dependent variable in my study is: _____

   I would describe it as follows *(circle the term in each set that applies)*:

   [quantitative or categorical] [nominal or ordinal or interval or ratio]

7. My study does not have independent/dependent variables. The variable(s) in my study is (are):

8. For *each* variable above that yields numerical data, I will treat it as follows *(check one in each column)*:

	INDEPENDENT	DEPENDENT	OTHER
Raw Score	_____	_____	_____
Age/grade equivalents	_____	_____	_____
Percentile	_____	_____	_____
Standard score	_____	_____	_____

9. I do not have any variables that yield numerical data in my study _____(√).

Problem Sheet 8: Instrument Validity and Reliability

1. Indicate any *existing* instruments you plan to use: _____
   _____
   _____

   I have learned the following about the validity and reliability of scores obtained
   with these instruments. _____
   _____
   _____

2. I plan to *develop* the following instruments:

   I will try to ensure reliability and validity of results obtained with these instruments
   by using one or more of the tips described on page 000:
   _____
   _____

3. For each instrument I plan to use:

   a. This is how I will check internal consistency:_____
   _____
   _____

   b. This is how I will check reliability over time (stability): _____
   _____
   _____

   c. This is how I will check validity: _____
   _____
   _____

Problem Sheet 9: Internal Validity

1. My question or hypothesis is: _____
   _____

2. I have placed an X in the blank in front of four of the threats listed below that apply
   to my study. I explain why I think each one is a problem and then explain how I
   would attempt to control for the threat.

THREATS: _____ Subject characteristics _____ Mortality   _____ Location

   _____ Instrumentation   _____ Testing   _____ History

   _____ Maturation   _____ Subject attitude _____ Regression

   _____ Implementation   _____ Other

Threat 1: _____ Why? _____

_____

I will control by _____

_____

Threat 2: _____ Why? _____

_____

I will control by _____

_____

Threat 3: _____ Why? _____

_____

I will control by _____

_____

Threat 4: _____ Why? _____

_____

I will control by _____

_____

Problem Sheet 10: Descriptive Statistics

1. The question or hypothesis of my study is: _____

2. My variables are: (1) _____

    (2) _____ (others) _____

3. I consider variable 1 to be: quantitative _____ categorical_____

4. I consider variable 2 to be: quantitative _____ categorical_____

5. I would summarize the results for each variable checked below *(indicate with a check mark):*

	Variable 1:	Variable 2:	Other:
a. Frequency polygon b. Five-number summary c. Box Plot d. Mean e. Median f. Percentages g. Standard deviation h. Frequency table i. Bar graph j. Pie Chart			

6. I would describe the relationship between variables 1 and 2 by *(indicate with a check mark):*

    a. Comparison of frequency polygons _____

    b. Comparison of averages _____

    c. Crossbreak table(s) _____

    d. Correlation coefficient _____

    e. Scatterplot _____

    f. Reporting of percentages _____

Problem Sheet 11: Inferential Statistics

1. The question or hypothesis of my study is: _____
   _____

2. The descriptive statistic(s) I would use to describe the relationship I am
   hypothesizing would be: _____
   _____

3. The appropriate inference technique for my study would be: _____
   _____

4. Circle the appropriate word in the sentences below.

   a. I would use a *parametric* or a *nonparametric* technique because: _____
   _____

   b. I *would* or *would not* do a significance test because: _____
   _____
   _____

   c. I *would* or *would not* calculate a confidence interval because: _____
   _____
   _____

5. The type of sample used in my study is: _____

6. The type of sample used in my study places the following limitation(s) on my use of
   inferential statistics:
   _____
   _____

Problem Sheet 12: Statistics in Perspective

1. The question or hypothesis of my study is: _____

   _____

2. My expected relationship(s) would be described using the following descriptive
   statistics: _____

   _____

   _____

   _____

   _____

3. The inferential statistics I would use are: _____

   _____

   _____

   _____

   _____

4. I would evaluate the magnitude of the relationship(s) I find by: _____

   _____

   _____

   _____

   _____

5. The changes (if any) in my use of descriptive or inferential statistics from those I
   described in Problem Sheets 10 and 11 are as follows: _____

   _____

   _____

   _____

   _____

   _____

   _____

Problem Sheet 13: Research Methodology

You should complete Problem Sheet 13 once you have decided which of the methodologies described in Chapters 13-17 and 19-24 you plan to use. You might wish to consider, however, whether your research question could be investigated by other methodologies.

1. The question or hypothesis of my study is: _____

_____

_____

2. The methodology I intend to use is: _____

_____

_____

3. A brief summary of what I intend to do, when, where, and how is as follows: _____

_____

_____

_____

_____

_____

_____

_____

_____

_____

4. The major problems I foresee at this point include the following: _____

_____

_____

_____

_____

_____

_____